To
PRESERVE
AND
PROTECT

{ The Life of Edwin Meese III }

To
Preserve
and
Protect

{ The Life of Edwin Meese III }

Lee Edwards

© 2005 by The Heritage Foundation
214 Massachusetts Avenue, NE
Washington, DC 20002-4999
(202) 546-4400
heritage.org

Printed in the United States of America.

ISBN 0-89195-116-4

Cover and interior book design by Carolyn Belefski

CONTENTS

~~

Foreword

by Edwin J. Feulner

~⁓

Our city, Washington, this center of power for the world, desperately needs more people like Ed Meese. The town is brimming over with men and women who strive for their own power for the sake of themselves. But even Ed Meese's enemies (whose public pronouncements show they know next to nothing about the kind of man Ed really is) are forced to admit that whatever their disagreements with him, he seems to be utterly devoid of personal ambition.

Who among Washington's power brokers has had more chances than Ed Meese to step into the limelight and grab something for himself? Instead, for all the years I've known him, Edwin Meese III has been about one thing: doing what he sees as the next right thing for America.

For years, that was serving Ronald Reagan in whatever capacity the Great Man needed him. Today it is serving as The Heritage Foundation's leading expert on a host of issues, including what should be done to bring our legal system back into line with limited government as set forth in the U.S. Constitution. The key word, in case you missed it (as his political enemies consistently do), is "serving."

Ed's accomplishments are well known, but you will find out much you didn't know about them between the covers of Lee Edwards's excellent book. The Heritage Foundation and I recently showed our appreciation for those accomplishments by bestowing upon Ed our highest award, the Clare Boothe Luce Award for Conservative Leadership in America and the world.

For me, the singular thing about Ed Meese is his utter humility, despite the awesome responsibilities God has seen fit to place in his hands.

I'll always remember several years ago, when we were planning the Heritage Christmas party, and we asked around for someone willing to play Santa. Ed responded. And when he came downstairs that evening, dressed in a Santa suit, I noticed something. Several Heritage families had brought their children to meet Santa. Instead of focusing on himself and laughing with his compatriots about the idea of Ed Meese in a Santa suit, Ed was occupied with something else: As always throughout his career, he had a job to do, and he was doing it. He was really playing Santa.

And after he'd given out gifts to the children, and it came time for a few gag gifts for some of our star staffers, I noticed something else: Ed had clearly taken a lot of time to prepare remarks that were funny and meaningful for each person receiving a gift. He delivered them flawlessly, and they had the effect Ed intended: We had a marvelous time.

This is the Ed Meese you will meet in these pages, between the great controversies and struggles and triumphs that have marked his career. And it is the Ed Meese I am privileged to call my friend.

INTRODUCTION

~⁓

When Ronald Reagan was once asked whom he would rely on if he faced a crisis, he replied without hesitation: "Ed Meese."[1] Reagan's ready response reveals the special relationship between one of the most successful presidents in modern history and his indispensable aide and policy adviser.

Time and again, Reagan would turn to Ed Meese after a far-ranging discussion among cabinet officers and policy experts. Meese, who as usual had been taking careful notes on a yellow legal pad, would present the arguments on all sides so scrupulously that no one objected. "No one could synthesize policy for the President as Ed did," remarks James A. Baker, chief of staff for President Reagan in his first term and a member of the famed White House "troika" of Baker, Meese and Michael K. Deaver. "He was superb."[2] "Reagan valued Ed's mind," says Deaver, "his ability to sum up and recommend."[3]

Reagan also valued Ed Meese's steadfast loyalty, not simply to himself but to conservative principles such as limited government, free enterprise, individual freedom, and strong moral values. "He tended the prairie fire" that Reagan ignited in California, says Deaver, who served as Meese's deputy in Sacramento, "and made sure it didn't go out."[4] The President used Meese as "a sounding board" for issues and ideas, according to William P. Clark, who preceded Meese as Governor Reagan's chief of staff and was later President Reagan's national security adviser. "Ed had an unsurpassed knowledge of the President's thinking."[5]

From their first days in Sacramento, Governor Reagan relied on Meese. Drawing on his years as deputy district attorney in Alameda County, which included the University of California at Berkeley, Meese helped organize a policy of firm response to campus and other disorders, a core issue for Reagan in his 1966 gubernatorial campaign. Meese developed a system for evaluating judicial candidates that removed "cronyism" from the courts—a frequent criticism of previous administrations—and ensured that California had highly qualified judges who "understood and believed in the law."[6]

In 1971, Meese suggested the establishment of a task force on welfare reform to isolate the causes of runaway state spending and design a new welfare system. The new program transformed public welfare in California—the welfare caseload dropped by several hundred thousand people while payments to the truly needy increased significantly. Reagan's welfare reform, as the veteran Washington analyst Allan Ryskind summed it up, "proved that conservative principles applied to a seemingly intractable domestic problem could be highly effective." Reagan biographer Lou Cannon called the California Welfare Reform Act "a seminal achievement of the Reagan governorship."[7]

In Washington, D.C., Presidential Counsellor Ed Meese, knowing Reagan's preference for cabinet government, devised an innovative

President Reagan consults with Meese in the Oval Office, circa 1981.

The White House

system of "cabinet councils" that grouped members according to their areas of responsibility. The five original councils were economic affairs, natural resources and the environment, commerce and trade, human resources, and national security. Added later were food and agriculture, legal policy, and management and administration.

A cabinet council, explained Martin Anderson, Reagan's chief domestic and economic policy adviser in his first two years, was "really a smaller, tailor-made version of the cabinet" with the "same force and authority in dealing" with issues that the entire cabinet had. Anderson estimated that "almost all of the policy work" during the first years of the Reagan Administration—including the historic Economic Recovery Tax Act of 1981—was funneled through the cabinet councils. Although overlooked by the Washington press at the time, the initiative was described by liberal academic Stuart E. Eizenstat, who served as President Jimmy Carter's domestic policy adviser, as "one of the more intriguing organizational efforts at cabinet-White House cooperation that we have seen in years."[8]

Ed Meese's responsibilities as principal policy adviser to President Reagan ran the gamut of issues from abortion to the "zero option" on intermediate-range nuclear missiles. In mid-September 1981, for example, he hosted a small meeting to discuss the feasibility of developing an anti-ballistic missile system in keeping with Reagan's long-expressed opposition to the U.S. policy of Mutual Assured Destruction (MAD). The group agreed that a system to intercept ballistic missiles in the earth's atmosphere and above was possible. After meeting again to explore provisional plans, Meese arranged a meeting with President Reagan on January 8, 1982. Reagan directed the National Security Council (NSC) staff to develop a proposal for a strategic defense program. Meese credits National Security Adviser William Clark with making sure this happened, along with the President's unwavering personal commitment. But it was Ed Meese's initiative that set in motion the process that culminated in Reagan's March 1983 announcement of the Strategic Defense Initiative (SDI) and helped convince the Kremlin it could not win an arms race.

As Presidential Counsellor and then Attorney General, Ed Meese played an essential role in creating the system by which jurists committed to judicial restraint and the written Constitution were selected. Reagan, explained Meese, wanted to name federal judges who would look at the Constitution and statute law and "expound their evident meaning" rather than use loopholes or convoluted logic to reach some "preconceived [socio-political] conclusion."[9] As Attorney General, Meese oversaw a team of experts who scrupulously vetted candidates for the federal bench. Meese sometimes conducted the final interview before passing on a judicial recommendation to the President.

Contrary to some reports, Reagan appointees were not asked about their political beliefs, but were questioned about their understanding of the Constitution and their philosophy of judicial practice. Over the course of his two terms in office, President Reagan appointed almost half of the federal judiciary. Observers, liberal and conservative, have given them high marks for their judicial performance and integrity. Reagan's judges, wrote legal scholar Sheldon Goldman, ranked above those of Carter, Ford, Nixon, and Johnson.[10] T. Kenneth Cribb, Jr., Meese's top aide in the White House and at the Justice Department, argues that "Reagan's second most important accomplishment, after winning the Cold War, was judicial selection."[11]

Ever loyal to the written Constitution, Attorney General Meese delivered major addresses that provoked a great debate about the most important document of our Republic. Speaking to the American Bar Association in July 1985 (and later that year to the Federalist Society), Meese argued that the Constitution must be interpreted in light of its original meaning and the common understanding of the Founding Fathers who ratified it. He called for a "Jurisprudence of Original Intention" consistent with the admonition of Chief Justice John Marshall that "the Constitution is a limitation on judicial power as well as executive and legislative."[12]

A Founding Father

Defenders of the notion that the Constitution is what judges say it is vehemently disagreed. Among them was Supreme Court Associate Justice William J. Brennan, Jr., who insisted that the Constitution should be continuously adapted "to cope with the problems of a developing America." Meese, however, stood with the prudential legal philosophy of Justice Felix Frankfurter, who although a political liberal, said, "As a member of this court, I am not justified in writing my private notions of policy into the Constitution." "Ed Meese was the founding father of original understanding," says Douglas Kmiec, professor of law at Pepperdine University and former dean of Catholic University of America's law school. "Everyone on the Supreme Court today is an originalist," Kmiec argues. "That was not the case," he says, "prior to Ed Meese."[13]

Appearing at Tulane University in October 1986, Meese delivered a forthright address about "the law of the Constitution" in which he argued, daringly, that the Supreme Court was not the sole arbiter of the Constitution. Other branches of the federal government, he said, had a vital role in deciding constitutional meaning or application within their proper spheres of authority. The Constitution, he said, is not the same thing as constitutional law. "To confuse the Constitution with judicial pronouncements," Meese stated, allows no standard by which to criticize and seek the overruling of "the derelicts of constitutional law"—cases such as *Dred Scott v. Sanford* and *Plessy v. Ferguson*.[14]

As the nation's top legal officer, and consistent with what he knew to be the views of the President, Ed Meese spoke out forcefully for those whose rights had long been overlooked or shunted aside.

He argued that the *Roe v. Wade* decision on abortion should be reversed. He cited the discriminatory nature of affirmative action and other civil rights proposals such as school busing. He described the American Civil Liberties Union as a "criminals' lobby" and called *Miranda v. Arizona* an "infamous decision." He fought drug abuse as chairman of the National Drug Policy Board—reinforcing First Lady Nancy Reagan's successful "Just Say No" campaign—and reacted against the prevalence of obscene materials and child pornography in communities by establishing the Obscenity Enforcement Unit in the Justice Department's Criminal Division.

Some say that Ed Meese's finest hour came on the "four-day weekend" of November 21-24, 1986, when he and three of his top aides conducted an investigation of a hitherto secret Administration initiative toward Iran. Concerned about conflicting stories within the Administration, Meese suggested to Reagan that someone needed to review "all aspects" of the Iran initiative so that the Administration could present "a comprehensive and accurate account." The President asked Meese to take on the assignment.

To their surprise and dismay, Meese and his assistants discovered a memo in the files of NSC staffer Lt. Col. Oliver North describing a plan to direct profits derived from arms transactions with Iran to support the Contras—the Nicaraguan freedom fighters. Support for the Nicaraguan resistance was one of the most hotly debated issues of the day. Iran was also a sensitive subject—Americans had not forgotten that the Iranian government had held fifty-two Americans hostage in the U.S. Embassy in Tehran for over a year. The combination of Iran and the Contras was an explosive and potentially highly damaging issue to the Administration. "We had to find out exactly what had happened," Meese later wrote.[15] And they did.

Based on interviews with Oliver North, National Security Adviser John Poindexter, former National Security Adviser Robert McFarlane, and others, the Meese team discovered that there had been "diversion" of Iranian arms money to the Contras. Only three people in the U.S. government had apparently known about the scheme—North, Poindexter, and McFarlane. When a shocked President Reagan was told on November 24 what had been uncovered, he ordered an immediate and complete disclosure, resulting in a full-scale press conference the following day. The Iran-Contra affair (some called it a "scandal") produced official investigations by the Tower Commission appointed by the President, by Congress, and by independent counsel Lawrence E. Walsh. While these inquiries unearthed some new data, Meese pointed out that "in major respects they confirmed the story that my staff and I had been able to piece together in less than seventy-six hours."[16]

Meese never doubted the potential gravity of Iran-Contra and characterized it as "a serious mistake by men who, in their zeal to advance legitimate national interests, took steps that were both unauthorized and unwise." Their extreme actions, he said, "damaged the Administration" and "agitated the country." But he denied the charge by liberal Democrats and others that Iran-Contra had brought about a "constitutional crisis" or that the actions of a few members of the Administration constituted a "threat to democratic government."[17] The Administration's handling of Iran-Contra demonstrated that the system of checks and balances instituted by the Founders of the Republic still worked. Still, one can speculate about the course of events if Ed Meese—at President Reagan's direction—had not acted as promptly and thoroughly as he did. Any attempt at a cover-up would have prompted the media to suggest a

Ronald Reagan Library

The Troika: President Reagan's senior White House staff, 1981:
James Baker, Ed Meese, Michael Deaver.

parallel with Watergate and encouraged congressional calls for impeachment of the President.

"Who knows what would have happened," asks Lee Liberman Otis, general counsel in the Department of Energy and a founder of the Federalist Society, "if the Contra diversion had not been revealed by the President and the White House? And it was Ed Meese who uncovered the truth." "Ed Meese saved the presidency twice," says Kenneth Cribb. "First, when he got presidential permission to get to the bottom of Iran-Contra, and second, when instead of leaking as most do in Washington, he publicly announced the full findings at a White House press conference."[18]

Because of Ed Meese's unwavering fidelity to President Reagan and a conservative agenda, he became a prime target of those who were adamantly opposed to what the President was trying to accomplish at home and abroad. Unable to block what they perceived as wrong and even dangerous policies, partisans vented their mounting frustration and anger on the President's right-hand man. They leaked ugly rumors about his supposed incompetence as presidential adviser. Often quoted was Reagan campaign aide John Sears's wisecrack that Ed Meese's briefcase resembled "a black hole"—anything that went into it never came out.

Critics held up his Senate confirmation to be Attorney General for over a year while an independent counsel picked and probed into alleged misdeeds such as a gift of "standard-issue" cuff links from the government of South Korea; whether Meese had been given preferential treatment in his promotion from lieutenant colonel to colonel in the Army Reserve; and the fact, admitted by Meese, that he had failed to list a $15,000 loan to his wife, Ursula, by a former associate on his financial disclosure statement. In his 385-page report, independent counsel Jake Stein said of every allegation that there was either "no basis for any criminal charge" or "no evidence of special treatment." President Reagan publicly declared that "it's always gratifying when the honor of a just man is vindicated, and that's exactly what has happened with the report of the Independent Counsel."[19]

With characteristic grace, Meese said he was "not bitter at all" about the lengthy investigation or the mudslinging, although some had dug deep for their mud. At his confirmation hearings, for example, Democratic Senator Patrick Leahy of Vermont had bitterly remarked, "The Senate, as presently constituted, would confirm Jack the Ripper as surgeon general if the president asked it to."[20] Rank partisanship did not prevail: The Senate confirmed Edwin Meese III as Attorney General by a margin of more than two to one.

Meese's forbearance seemed to enrage his critics. In May 1987, congressional Democrats urged an investigation of whether Meese, while in the White House, had received anything of value in exchange for asking that the Army consider the application of a company whose legal counsel was a long-time friend of his. Such referrals, of course, occur frequently in the federal government, especially in Congress. A year later, independent counsel James McKay announced that no "evidence [was] discovered that Mr. Meese, at any time, knowingly received any money or thing of value from anyone in return for or on account of any official act he performed which benefited the company." Regarding other allegations, including "lost" stocks and late tax payments, McKay reported: "The financial records of Mr. and Mrs. Meese did not evidence any unexplained income or expenditure, unusual asset, concealed transaction or any other unexplained improvement in their financial condition since 1980."[21]

That should have ended the matter, but when Ed Meese resigned as Attorney General in August 1988, his ideological enemies and those of the President rushed to condemn him and his record. According to Norman Dorsen, president of the American Civil Liberties Union, Meese had "presided over the Reagan administration's efforts to restrict the individual liberties of millions of Americans." Ed Meese "has never been more than two steps ahead of the law," said Arthur J. Kropp, president of the liberal lobbying group People for the American Way. "He leaves a record of shame." "He's been a disaster as attorney general," said Hazel Dukes, president of the New York chapter of the NAACP.[22] When polled by *The Wall Street Journal*, Harvard professor Arthur M. Schlesinger, Jr., radical leftist Victor Navasky, and liberal columnist Hodding Carter III placed Meese among the "worst" Reagan appointees. Carter called Meese "consistently wrong" in his advice and of "dubious" ethics.[23]

And yet those who had worked with Ed Meese over a lifetime of public service showered him with encomiums that would make a mother blush. "His tenacious pursuit of the criminal element both in this country and abroad," says William Bradford Reynolds, Assistant Attorney General for Civil Rights during the Reagan Administration, "strengthened and better focused the [Justice Department's] law enforcement mission." "He has pulled together the conservative public interest legal movement as no one else could have done," says Edwin J. Feulner, President of The Heritage Foundation, referring to a seminal accomplishment of Meese in his post-Reagan Administration career. Ed Meese, says former Secretary of Defense Caspar Weinberger, was "always one of the most effective and believable spokesmen" during "the eight great years of Ronald Reagan's presidency." It was Ed Meese, points out California state judge Lois Haight, who set up the task force on victims of crime that resulted in "federal crime legislation and laws in fifty states protecting victims."[24]

Whether they had known him for forty years or four, the tributes of Meese's colleagues were remarkably similar. "You could always depend upon Ed," remarks Reagan aide and speechwriter Peter Hannaford, "for a well-reasoned conservative response to almost any issue." "He was sane, solid, reliable," says campaign aide Jeffrey Bell. "People missed him when he wasn't there." "He had an uncanny ability to look down the road," says Pendleton James, who was asked by Meese to start working on the presidential transition even before Reagan was nominated by the Republican Party in July 1980. "Ed loved ideas," says Charles Cooper, former head of the Office of Legal Counsel, who helped organize a series of Justice Department conferences on everything from the First Amendment to federalism at Meese's instruction. "He wanted to explore them to their deepest level."

"Ed's first and only interest was in serving the President," asserts Richard Wirthlin, Reagan's pollster and political strategist. "When he left the White House for Justice there was a hole that was never completely filled." "He never seemed to be thrown off balance by stress or by things going the wrong way," says Theodore Olson, who served as head of the Office of Legal Counsel in Reagan's first term and Solicitor General for President George W. Bush. "He created an environment," says John Richardson, who served as Meese's chief of staff at Justice, "where everyone felt free to propose and advocate new ideas. He had convictions of iron, but an open mind." "What was most extraordinary about Ed," says Mark Levin, head of the Landmark Legal Foundation, who also served as his chief of staff at Justice, "was how he functioned so efficiently despite the vicious efforts of the Left to destroy him."[25]

One reason he did was the President's steadfast support. During the McKay inquiry, when questions were raised by political opponents and the media about the integrity of his Attorney General, Ronald Reagan responded, "If Ed Meese is not a good man, there are no good men."[26]

Where, then, did this good man come from? This indispensable man who never wavered in his commitment to the Reagan Revolution, who never seemed to lose his temper or his sense of humor regardless of the crisis, who never said an unkind word about anyone, even those who heaped calumny on him. Supreme Court Justice Clarence Thomas commented to his wife, Ginni, that of all the people they knew in Washington, Ed Meese most nearly "epitomizes Jesus Christ," by reason of his grace and poise in the most trying of times and his abiding concern for others, not himself. "He's a great man," remarks Ginni Thomas, "but he walks with humility."[27] Who and what shaped the man whom his close colleague called "the perfect public servant"?

Chapter I
GROWING UP GOOD

~~

There have been Meeses in Oakland, California, since the city was founded in 1852. Herman Meese, Ed Meese's great-grandfather, was a skilled cabinetmaker who moved from San Francisco to Oakland in 1878 and helped establish the Zion Lutheran Church there. He was the first president of the congregation. Herman was among the German Lutherans who came to America seeking freedom from religious rationalism. They belonged to the Missouri Synod, a conservative branch of the Lutheran Church that believes in the Holy Scriptures as the inspired word of God and practices closed communion. They also believe in education and created the second-largest parochial school system in America.

Edwin Meese, Sr., Ed Meese's grandfather, attended a Lutheran college in Fort Wayne, Indiana, and went into the insurance business. He began the Meese tradition of public service in Oakland by serving as city councilman and city treasurer at the turn of the twentieth century. He was also president of the Zion Lutheran congregation. His younger son was Edwin Meese, Jr., Ed Meese's father, who attended the University of California (not yet known as Berkeley) as an undergraduate and as a law student. Ed Junior began a long career in Oakland city government in the 1920s, first as principal assistant to a state senator, then clerk of the police court for twenty years, next chief deputy tax collector, and finally tax collector and treasurer of Alameda County for twenty-four years—the latter a non-partisan but elected position. Preserving another family tradition, he too served as president of the Zion Lutheran Church.

"Family and patriotism were quite important to my parents," said Ed Meese, Jr. "Because my parents cared about these things, I did too. Not that we were zealots, always trying to show our badge of patriotism. But we just did things that came naturally to us. If there's a holiday, we fly the flag."[28] Too old for active military service in World War II (he had been a private in World War I), Ed Meese, Jr., joined the Coast Guard Reserve and became a member of the Volunteer Port Security Force that helped guard the Port of Oakland. Without complaint, he took the 8 p.m. to 2 a.m. shift several times a week. In war and peace, he was a community leader, serving as president of the Kiwanis Club, commander of the American Legion, chairman of the Alameda County Red Cross, and a leader of the Boy Scouts.

Into his eighties, Edwin Junior would tell visitors compelling stories about growing up in turn-of-the-century California, especially his memory of the 1906 San Francisco earthquake. "The sky across the bay glowed orange from the fire after the earthquake struck," he told one reporter. San Francisco was closed, but his father had gotten a pass from the governor to enter the city, and ten-year-old Ed Meese, Jr., went with him. "We stood there and looked down on what was left of San Francisco. The city was still smoldering.... That was the first time I ever saw my father with tears in his eyes."[29]

The Meese boys, circa 1941: Clifford, Myron, Ed, and George.

Ed Meese's mother, Leone, readily acknowledged the strong influence of their Lutheran faith on her four sons. (Edwin III, born
on December 2, 1931, was the oldest.) But she believed their father
was more important, calling him "the most marvelous example."[30]
The Meeses were as patriotic as they were pious, wrote one chronicler—"exemplars of the Protestant American ethic."[31] Every night
the family knelt and prayed together. Every night they stood to say
the Pledge of Allegiance. Theirs was a quiet but deep affection. "We
kiss 'hello' or 'goodbye' and that's it," said Leone Meese. "We know
we love each other. That's the important thing."[32] In good times and
bad, they sustained each other. Ed shared a room with his brother
Myron, who was born with spina bifida that left him partially para-
lyzed. But Myron was included in every family activity—and was

there when the Meese family met President Reagan in the Oval Office of the White House in early 1981.

Growing up in Oakland, Ed and his brothers earned their spending money the old-fashioned way—by their own effort. Ed had a paper route as soon as he could ride a bicycle, and also worked in a drug store. During his teens he received $2.50 a day clearing trails in the rugged East Bay park system. Young Ed was always bursting with energy: When just ten, he and his younger brothers published a mimeographed neighborhood newspaper, *The Weekly Herald*, and used the profits to buy a war bond. He became a Cub Scout and then a Boy Scout.

Ed was very close to his father, who early on inspired him to consider a career in law enforcement. Leone Meese remembered her husband coming home from his job as police court clerk and recounting dramatic stories about the day's proceedings to their oldest son. In high school, Ed satisfied his desire for courtroom forensics by joining the debating team and leading it to victory in city and state competitions. "He was a terrific debater," remembers his wife, Ursula, who was one year behind him at Oakland High School and joined the Forensic Society to be near her future husband. Ed Meese learned to present succinctly all sides of an argument—a skill he put to good use as Ronald Reagan's aide decades later.

In the spring of 1949, Ed graduated from Oakland High as valedictorian. He had applied to and been accepted by Stanford—which was prohibitively expensive—and the University of California at Berkeley, which offered him a small scholarship. There was another but distant possibility. At the suggestion of the board of the Junior Statesman School—a six-week summer program at Montezuma Mountain School in the Santa Cruz Mountains that he had attend-

Ed Meese, Oakland High School valedictorian, class of 1949.

ed the previous year—he had also applied to Yale, "something almost unimaginable for a boy from California," Meese says. "Out of the blue," he remembers, "two weeks before I was graduated, I was accepted by Yale and got a scholarship" to study political science in New Haven. Although the idea of traveling 3,000 miles from home was "somewhat daunting," the Oakland youngster headed east, accompanied by his high school debate partner Robert Cowell, who had also won a scholarship.[33]

While earning a B.A., Ed Meese found the time to serve as president of the Yale Political Union, chairman of the Yale Debating Association, manager of the track team, cadet commander of the ROTC, president of the Lutheran Student Association, and vice president for the northeast division of the National Lutheran Student Association. He also made the dean's list, a fact omitted in a major profile published years later by a leading California newspaper. The paper erroneously wrote that Meese had been "a mediocre student" at Yale.[34] "My favorite instructor," he recalls, "was Chuck Lichenstein," who later served as Ambassador Jeane Kirkpatrick's chief deputy at the United Nations and then became a senior fellow at The Heritage Foundation. Lichenstein's class was

Local Government.[35]

Upon entering Yale, Meese had enrolled in the ROTC and later also enlisted in the Army Reserve as a private first class. He had admired the military from his boyhood during World War II, influenced by his father's volunteer service and inspired by the military motto, "Duty, Honor, Country." Upon graduation from Yale in 1953, he was commissioned a second lieutenant in the field artillery but was not immediately called up. He decided to enroll in law school at UC-Berkeley, and had completed his first year at Boalt Hall when he was called into active duty.

Ed Meese spent twenty-four months at Fort Sill, Oklahoma—working with the 240 mm Howitzer, one of the largest artillery pieces in the Army—and was eventually assigned as assistant battalion operations officer. The experience ignited a lifelong interest in logistics and organization. "We used twenty-ton cranes to emplace the 240. I was responsible for the bulldozers and other equipment. It was all part of an education I would never receive at any other time in my life."[36] Still a second lieutenant, he was given a major's responsibilities in Exercise Sagebrush, one of the largest peacetime exercises of the 1950s, covering half of Louisiana, before completing his active duty in June 1956. He continued in the Army Reserve, specializing in military intelligence, and rose to the rank of colonel before retiring in early 1984, when he was nominated as Attorney General.

Upon his return to Berkeley's Boalt Hall in 1956, Meese continued to display his forensic skills. He won the Moot Court Prize in his second year and was elected to the Moot Court Board the following year, becoming its vice chairman. That same year, he won the state Moot Court championship. A classmate described him as an "all-American, Jack Armstrong guy" who wore white shirts and had a crew cut.[37] Although his grades were admittedly not "great" (he worked full-time during his last two years of law school), Ed Meese was almost elected valedictorian by the Boalt class of 1958. Fulfilling his long-held ambition, he joined the district attorney's office of Alameda County in October 1958 as a law clerk at the munificent salary of $281 a month. He passed the bar the following January and became a deputy district attorney for Alameda County. He even got a raise—to $400 a month.

Soon after, in September 1959, Ed Meese married his high school sweetheart Ursula (Ursie) Herrick, whose father was Oakland's postmaster. "It was a whirlwind courtship of eleven years," remarks Ursula wryly. The wedding reception was held in the officers' club on Treasure Island in San Francisco Bay, and they cut the cake with a military sword. It was a union of similar backgrounds and interests—each came from a close-knit devout family (the Herricks were Episcopalian) that believed in public service. Ursula was as smart as she was pretty. Voted "the outstanding senior woman" at the College of the Pacific, she enrolled in a one-year graduate program in business at Harvard-Radcliffe. She returned home to begin work as a deputy probation officer in Oakland, but she had something else on her mind and in her heart. "I knew I should marry Ed in high school," Ursula recalls. "He probably had that intention, too."[38]

They began their honeymoon at Lake Tahoe, Nevada, but on the second day, snow was forecasted, and, as Ursula says, "Ed hates snow." "Why don't we go to Los Angeles where the sun's shining," suggested the bridegroom, "and while we're there we can visit the new police department building?" The bride smilingly agreed, and thus was born the myth that Ed and Ursula Meese spent their honeymoon in a Los

Angeles police car. While it is true they visited the L.A. Police Headquarters, they were in Disneyland the following day, happily explor-
ing Sleeping Beauty's castle and the wonders of the deep in Captain
Nemo's submarine. But, Ursula Meese readily admits, her husband
"can't drive by a police or fire department without slowing down."[39]

Berkeley Blows Up

Over the next three years, Ed Meese prosecuted a wide variety of
felony cases—including capital crimes—while being allowed, because of his modest salary, to maintain a small private practice at
night and on the weekends. He limited himself to civil law—mostly
wills and probate. "Ed was one of the most highly organized, le-
gally capable people you'll ever want to see," said fellow deputy
district attorney Lowell Jensen, who later became Alameda D.A.
"Sometimes he maybe had too many things going on at once—here
and on the outside. But he kept them all going well."[40] Meese
impressed his boss Frank Coakley so much that he was picked to
represent the California District Attorneys Association and the
California Peace Officers Association at the 1961 general session
of the state legislature in Sacramento and again at the 1962 budget
session of the legislature. He helped draft statutes on narcotics control and rehabilitation and served on statewide committees dealing
with law enforcement legislation, public safety, and administration
of criminal justice. Among those who took note of Ed Meese's quiet efficiency was Republican State Senator Donald Grunsky, who
would later recommend him for a position with Governor-elect
Ronald Reagan.

But first came a series of events that "plunged the UC-Berkeley campus into a crisis unprecedented in American higher education."[41] Students returning to campus in September 1964 encountered an impassioned "Letter to Undergraduates" that urged them to "organize and split this campus wide open!" Demands included the immediate abolition of undergraduate grades and a permanent student role in the running of the university.

The conflict between the students and the university administration climaxed in early December at a giant evening rally and sit-in at Sproul Hall, which contained the offices of the president and other university officials. An alarmed Chancellor Edward Strong called in Berkeley police and other law enforcement agencies to clear the hall, and 773 people were arrested. Several hundred professors protested, calling for the dismissal of all charges against the demonstrators. The university president attempted to negotiate a ceasefire, but the radicals were interested in perpetuating conflict rather than resolving it. The Free Speech Movement morphed into the Filthy Speech Movement, "a loose alliance of radical students, hippies, and street people" that kept alive the spirit of protest at UC-Berkeley for the rest of the decade.[42]

A leader in the campaign to restore order to the Berkeley campus—*his* old campus and that of his father—was Ed Meese. Democratic Governor Edmund (Pat) Brown, who had known Meese when he was the legislative representative for district attorneys and police officers in Sacramento, telephoned him the night of the mass sit-in to ask how best to resolve the crisis. Meese did not mince words. "I told him," he recalled later, "that the people in the building should be arrested and taken out of there. I told him that if they were allowed to stay, there would be another mob scene, even bigger, the next day."[43] A reluctant Brown agreed, and under Meese's supervision and that of Deputy District Attorney Lowell Jensen, the police cleared the building, taking into custody hundreds of young men and women. Meese and Jensen were co-counsels in the mass trial of the Berkeley demonstrators.

Liberals accused Brown of overreacting, but the majority of Californians praised the use of prudential force to defuse a potentially dangerous situation. Ed Meese emerged from the Berkeley crisis as "the law-and-order man" who over the next two years refined the techniques of dealing with mass demonstrations. In recognition of his leadership, he was named one of the five Outstanding Young Men of California (along with baseball great Willie Mays) by the California Junior Chamber of Commerce. The Jaycees were undoubtedly impressed by the long list of Ed Meese's activities outside the D.A.'s office: member of the Army Intelligence Reserve, president of the Junior Statesman Foundation, secretary-treasurer of the Criminal Courts Association of Alameda County, and a member of the U.S. Supreme Court Bar, the American Bar Association, the Peace Officers Association of California, and the Reserve Officers Association.

When confronted with anti-Vietnam war protests in 1965 and 1966—including the burning of draft cards and other disruptive acts—Meese used on-the-scene intelligence to isolate and arrest the ringleaders, demoralizing their followers. He counseled early morning arrests when there were smaller crowds and fewer reporters. Under his supervision, wrote one newspaper, arresting officers "for the first time" used Polaroid cameras to take photos of demonstrators, settling any question at a trial about the defendant's involvement and eliminating the need to take large numbers of people to a police station for booking.⁴⁴ Meese also championed the co-ordinated use of different law enforcement agencies—such as the Sheriff's Department, the local police, and the National Guard—to put down civil disturbances.

Ed Meese insisted there was nothing personal in his commitment to arresting and prosecuting the disrupters—he was only doing his duty to keep the peace and protect the people of Alameda County. He was upset, however, by antiwar demonstrators who burned the American flag while American soldiers were fighting in Vietnam. "Those demonstrations," he asserted years later, "prolonged the war and cost a lot of American lives."⁴⁵ And he made it clear he would not tolerate the gun-toting Black Panthers who called the police "pigs" and threatened all-out war against the "honkie" power structure.

There was an affinity between Meese and the cop on the beat—he collected small model squad cars and statuettes of "pigs" (the radicals' favorite epithet for the police). A standing joke in the Alameda County courthouse was that Meese would drop everything and respond to a call coming in over his desktop police radio. But as fellow deputy district attorney Jensen explained, "It was a regular practice for us to ride with them on patrol." Such rides had a purpose. "D.A.s could help educate the police about exclusionary law," Jensen said, and D.A.s got "good feedback from police to help our job."⁴⁶

And so when Governor-elect Ronald Reagan, who had promised to "clean up the mess" on the campuses and faced sixty men on condemned row, began looking for someone to be his secretary for extradition and clemency (the title was soon changed to legal affairs secretary), Senator Grunsky among others suggested that he consider the thirty-five-year-old deputy district attorney in Alameda County who had shown his mettle during the tumultuous

UC-Berkeley student demonstrations.

Ed Meese had never been political—he thought of himself as a disinterested public servant like his father, who was elected six times to the non-partisan office of Alameda County treasurer. "We have a responsibility to our country to give it the best we can," explained Ursula Meese, expressing the attitude of her own family as well as that of her husband, "to work in public service if you have the talent to give."[47] When Ed Meese got a telephone call in December 1966 inviting him to interview for a job with the governor-elect, he recalls, "I was not particularly interested."[48] He saw himself as staying in his hometown and probably eventually becoming Alameda County district attorney. And Ursula had little desire to move the family, which now included six-year-old Michael, four-year-old Scott, and four-month-old Dana, from their comfortable home in Oakland.

But Meese was curious to hear more about Reagan's plans to strengthen law enforcement in California. He traveled to Sacramento, where members of Reagan's transition team described his prospective duties as a legal assistant to the governor and discussed the post at a salary of $16,500 a year. He was still uncertain until he talked personally with Ronald Reagan. "I was impressed," Meese remembers, "by how much he knew and how our ideas on capital punishment and campus disturbances complemented each other." After a half hour, says Meese, "he offered me the job and I accepted on the spot. There wasn't a doubt in my mind that this was the man I wanted to work for."[49]

Chapter II

ASSISTING THE GOVERNOR

~~

Ronald Reagan governed California as if he were the chairman of the board of a large, a very large, corporation. If it had been a company, California's economy would have placed it at the top of the Fortune 500, second only to General Motors. Reagan persuaded business and professional men to give up large salaries and work in his administration at a considerable financial sacrifice. He relied upon department heads and assistants to handle the details and allow him to concentrate on key issues such as cutting taxes, reducing wasteful spending, restoring order on the campuses, and appointing judges of the highest caliber. He was determined to deliver on his campaign promise to foster a "creative society" that would mobilize the full resources of all the people and "start a prairie fire that will sweep the nation and prove we are number one in more than size and crime and taxes."[50] And he did.

When Reagan became governor in January 1967, California was spending a million dollars more each day than it was taking in. When he left office in December 1974, he turned over to his successor a surplus of $554 million. Under Reagan, California's bonds were upgraded to the highest possible rating—Moody's Triple-A—for the first time in thirty-one years. "We exaggerate very little," editorialized the *San Francisco Examiner*, "when we say that [Reagan] has saved the state from bankruptcy."[51]

At the same time, Reagan was the biggest tax-cutter in the state's history, enacting over $5.7 billion in tax relief, despite an almost $1 billion tax increase in his first year—an increase necessitated by the state constitutional requirement that the budget be balanced every year. His measures included the first comprehensive property tax relief program in California history, the elimination of taxes on families earning less than $8,000 a year, the reduction of taxes on lower-to-middle wage earners, and reduction of the business inventory tax by half. "California is in good financial shape today," stated the veteran legislative analyst A. Alan Post at the end of Reagan's second term, "because Reagan gave it a sound tax base."[52]

The size of state government, as measured by the number of employees, was held to a near standstill. A determined Reagan resisted the big spenders all the way, vetoing 994 bills, with only one veto being overridden. "There is solid evidence," wrote the *Los Angeles Times*, "that Reagan, particularly through his vetoes, [was] an effective brake in keeping government spending from accelerating at an even more rapid rate."[53] In his first term, Reagan also restored use of the death penalty for capital crimes and provided stiffer penalties against such crimes as rape and robbery, instituted tuition at the state university system, and created the first state department of consumer affairs. He also established a cabinet system of government so that no important decision was made without first discussing it in detail at a cabinet meeting and then seeking and obtaining consensus. His predecessor, Pat Brown, had eight agency chiefs overseeing the state's twenty-three departments; Reagan cut the number of agencies in half.

To facilitate meetings, chief of staff William Clark created the one-page memorandum to be used by every cabinet officer and senior staff member. It was divided into four parts—issues, facts, discussion (pro and con), and recommendation. At first there were objections that complicated topics could not be so drastically condensed, but everyone discovered that reducing his thoughts to a single page required him to eliminate the extraneous and present the essentials of an issue. In the Reagan Administration, short was beautiful.

As he had pledged during the campaign, Governor Reagan acted decisively to quell campus lawlessness, tightening laws against unlawful assembly, suspending state financial support of students convicted of campus disturbances, and making it a crime to coerce the officials or teachers of any educational institution. Reagan emphasized that he was not seeking to deny academic freedom to anyone but to protect the rights of the law-abiding majority on campus. "Preservation of free speech," he said sternly, "does not justify letting beatniks and advocates of sexual orgies, drug usage and 'filthy speech' disrupt the academic community and interfere with our universities' purpose of learning and research."[54]

Many people contributed to Governor Reagan's effectiveness and success during his eight years in Sacramento, but one person became so essential that the press teasingly referred to him as the "assistant governor." Ed Meese, according to journalists Bob Schieffer and Gary Paul Gates and other observers, "rose quickly in rank and prominence" because he did his work quietly and efficiently and treated the governor with respect.[55] As legal affairs secretary, he worked out of a tiny office and on the supposedly "narrow" issues of clemency and extradition. But after every "deep discussion" among the governor's staff, he would ask, "Has anyone bothered to check the law?"[56] In very short order, Meese was given that responsibility. A strong advocate of the death penalty, he urged Reagan in 1967 to resist public pressure to stay the execution of Aaron Mitchell, who had been convicted of killing a policeman. Reagan took his advice and later said he appreciated how Meese had stood firm in the face of other advisers who had recommended clemency.

Ed Meese became the point man for the governor's law-and-order campaign against student disorders and other acts of civil disobedience. In October 1968, while still legal secretary, he prepared a memo for Bill Clark stating that the "disturbances and disruptions" on various campuses "cannot be allowed to continue and interfere with the proper functioning and the educational activities of these institutions."[57] In the spring of 1969, following the fire bombing of Wheeler Hall at Berkeley, the vandalizing of a dozen buildings, and the discovery of fire bombs, Reagan declared a state of emergency. "I am duty bound," he explained, "to make available all the force at my command to protect the rights of the people"—including the right of teachers and students "to learn without fear of violence or threat of violence."[58] The bond between the governor and the young legal secretary strengthened, and in 1969, when Bill Clark was named to a judgeship, thirty-eight-year-old Meese replaced him as chief of staff—at Clark's recommendation. "Five people wanted my job," recalls Clark. "Clearly the right person was Ed."[59]

One of Ed Meese's very first moves was to telephone Michael Deaver, Clark's deputy, who had become one of the governor's— and Nancy Reagan's—most trusted confidants. "I can't do this without you," Deaver recalls Meese saying.[60] When Meese asked

Meese and California Governor Ronald Reagan's Cabinet, 1969.

him to stay on as the number two man, Deaver agreed, and thus was forged a professional relationship that served Ronald Reagan superbly as governor and president over the next two decades.

The new chief of staff continued Bill Clark's practice of "round-tabling" issues, examining them from all points of view, before presenting them to the governor. He also understood, wrote Reagan biographer Lou Cannon, that Reagan wanted "tangible accomplishments," even if they fell short of conservative goals. As governor and as president, Reagan would accept seventy percent of what he asked for if he could come back later for the other thirty percent. Meese had "a unique ability," Cannon confirmed, to explain intricate issues to Reagan, avoiding legalisms and using stories and anecdotes to make a point just as Reagan did. Because he knew what Governor Reagan wanted to accomplish and never advocated his own agenda, Meese could speak for him with authority. Cannon once referred to Meese as "Reagan's geographer"—someone who drew maps of Reagan's world and chartered courses that enabled the governor to reach his destination.[61]

Meese was also "a good in-betweener," said Republican Robert Monagan, who briefly served as Assembly speaker in the Reagan years. "He understood the Legislature. He brought to his job an appreciation of government." Echoing other legislators, Monagan said, "You could trust Ed Meese. You never had to worry about him double-dealing with you."[62] As Reagan's chief formulator of policy after an easy 1970 reelection, Meese was generally praised for his grasp of the issues, his ability to guide a problem through the political shoals and, above all, his skills as a conciliator—firm but fair. "Meese was the most substantial factor," said former Republican assemblyman William Bagley, "in shifting the governor's office into governmental gear." "Were I in the governor's seat," conceded Bob Moretti, the Democratic speaker of the Assembly in Reagan's second term, "I would want someone like [Ed Meese] on my side."[63]

In an interview with the authoritative *California Journal*, Meese described his major functions as finding the right people for positions, setting priorities, promoting communications within the staff, and keeping the governor informed. "We had a lot of open decision making," he explained, "to avoid having people see who could buttonhole the Governor last" and try to persuade him to accept their position. Drawing upon his coaching experience as a recreation leader, Meese suggested that his job was "kind of like being the coach of a football team, and making sure that you've got the right person in the right position and that the right plays are being called."[64] But he stressed that the governor and not he determined the game plan. Cognizant of the enormous power inherent in his position, Meese said that his personal philosophy was that "the more power you have potentially, the more you have an obligation to utilize restraint when you exercise the power."[65]

Because Reagan preferred to act as "chairman of the board," Ed Meese served as coordinator of the cabinet sessions, usually attended by about twenty people. He was calm, deliberative, and humorous when necessary. Everyone was allowed to enter into the discussion, but at a certain point, Meese would say, "I think we've heard enough," and would summarize the arguments. His crisp summaries invariably brought the issue at hand into focus. Sometimes Reagan would make a decision right then, stating, "This is our policy," but often he would say, "I'd like to sleep on this. Let's take it up at the next meeting." As a result of Reagan's preference for cabinet government, everyone knew what everybody else was doing. There were not the mysteries and rumors that give rise to power struggles and internecine plotting. "Our administration, due to Ed," Reagan later said, "was more free of petty jealousies and bickering than in anything I've ever seen."[66]

To get the job done, Ed Meese arrived early and left late. The cabinet would meet regularly for breakfast before cabinet meetings to consider the day's agenda. "I remember one day," he recalled, "[when] we got together initially at six o'clock because we had to have a pre-meeting before the [breakfast] meeting at seven o'clock, in order to be ready for the Cabinet meeting at eight o'clock, and by nine o'clock we had the thing solved."[67] There were also after-hours cabinet meetings—in the chief of staff's office—when each cabinet member (if he was in town) would discuss whatever special problems he had had that day. Meese would take notes, and the following morning he would report to the governor. Thus was shaped a governing style in which Reagan did not involve himself in tactical decisions but was kept informed of the progress toward the policy goals of his administration. He personally and frequently intervened when necessary, as he did with reform of the state's assistance programs.

"Number One" Priority

Even before Reagan had promised welfare reform in his reelection campaign, Meese had begun working on it. As early as September 1968, in a cabinet-staff meeting, he argued that California should not allow the federal government "to tell us how or when to invoke [welfare] eligibility.... We should be able to develop our own procedures and not be barred from using our own methods." On August 4, 1970, a confidential memo drafted by Meese was sent under Reagan's name to members of the governor's cabinet and the senior staff. Announcing a study of the state's public assistance and education programs, the memo said: "This study will place heavy emphasis on the tax-payer as opposed to the tax-taker; on the truly needy as opposed to the lazy unemployable; on the student as opposed to educational frills; on basic needs as opposed to unmanageable enrichment programs; on measurable results as opposed to blind faith that an educator can do no wrong."[68]

Seeking recommendations for administrative action and legislation, the memo concluded, "I am determined to reduce these programs to essential services at a cost the taxpayer can afford to pay. This is our NUMBER ONE priority. We must bring all our resources to bear on this endeavor.... If we fail, no one ever again will be able to try. We must succeed."[69] Reagan summed up his view about welfare in a TV debate: "I believe that the government is supposed to *promote* the general welfare—I don't think it is supposed to *provide* it."[70]

There was good reason to be alarmed about the explosive growth of the state welfare program, particularly Aid to Families with Dependent Children (AFDC). In 1963, there were 375,000 AFDC recipients in California. When Reagan took office in 1967, the number had doubled to 769,000. By December 1969, shortly after Ed Meese became executive secretary or chief of staff, the AFDC rolls listed 1,150,687. A year later, a month after Reagan's reelection, there were 1,566,000 people on the AFDC list, nearly one out of every thirteen Californians. The caseload was increasing by 40,000 a month, and Finance Director Verne Orr warned that a continuing increase of this kind would bust the budget in 1972.

In response to the crisis and at Meese's suggestion, Reagan formed the Welfare Reform Task Force that put together the program that transformed public welfare in California and eventually throughout the nation. Among the changes: penalties were stiffened for welfare fraud; recipients with jobs were removed from the welfare rolls when their outside income exceeded 150 percent of their basic needs; adult children were required to contribute to the support of their aged parents on welfare; the power of counties to make absent fathers pay for the support of their families was broadened; and able-bodied recipients were required to take job training or work on public works projects at least four hours a day.

The results in California were dramatic. By September 1974, the total caseload had dropped by approximately 20 percent, but benefits to those without any outside income had risen by 41 percent. The dollar savings in the first two years were an estimated $1 billion. Even Reagan's Democratic successor, Jerry Brown (son of former Governor Pat Brown), was impressed, commenting, "Considering today's high unemployment, it is amazing that [the Reagan welfare program] has kept welfare down as much as it has."[71]

The Democratic legislature, dominated by liberals beholden to the welfare establishment, strongly resisted the proposed changes. But Reagan asked the people through a series of television and radio addresses to let their legislators know how they felt about reducing the number of people on welfare but increasing the support for those who truly needed help. One day, Assembly Speaker Robert Moretti appeared at Governor Reagan's office door and, holding up his hands, said, "Stop the cards and letters. I'm ready to negotiate a welfare reform act."[72]

A compromise on welfare reform was reached during five days of intense negotiations personally led by Reagan and Moretti, followed by six days of additional discussion of the details by the governor's aides and state legislators. The Reagan team was led by Meese, state welfare director Robert Carleson, legislative liaison George Steffes, and James Hall, secretary of the State Health and Welfare Agency. But the key role, wrote Lou Cannon, was played by Meese, "who won the respect of the Democratic negotiators" as the administration official who spoke most reliably for the governor and who had a realistic sense of how the game of politics was played in Sacramento.[73]

Every political administration has its accomplishments, large and small. Welfare reform was the most significant accomplishment of the Reagan Administration with an enduring national impact. Its success transformed Reagan from a celebrity governor grounded in conservative philosophy into "a high-performing chief of state and a credible presidential candidate."[74]

An important by-product of the Reagan initiative was the formation of the first freedom-based public interest law organization. California's entrenched welfare establishment, including legal aid societies and taxpayer-funded public interest law firms, fought the governor's changes every inch of the way. It was clear that a serious imbalance existed in the public interest law field. In mid-1972, members of the Reagan welfare reform legal team began meeting with other Administration officials, including Ed Meese, to talk about a new kind of nonprofit/general purpose public interest law firm that would litigate in support of the free enterprise system and private property rights. The following January, a group of prominent Californians from each of the state's six regions met in San Francisco. Ronald A. Zumbrun, a senior attorney in the state department of public works, was asked to develop a formal proposal which was adopted in February.

The new organization was incorporated as the Pacific Legal Foundation. Business leader John Simon Fluor was elected chairman of the board and started raising funds. Zumbrun was subsequently named PLF's president and CEO. The importance of Reagan's role can be seen in the fact that eleven of the first individuals to join the foundation's staff had been part of the welfare reform team. Today there are more than thirty conservative public interest law groups nationwide, each motivated by a respect for the Constitution and opposed to the radical agenda of the liberal establishment.

One of Reagan's few gubernatorial defeats occurred in November

1973 with his sponsorship of Proposition 1, an amendment to the state constitution that would have eventually placed a ceiling of seven percent on the income tax that the state could levy on its citizens. The amendment was drafted by Frank Walton, Reagan's secretary of business and transportation, and Lewis K. Uhler, director of the state Office of Economic Opportunity and former Meese classmate from the University of California law school. Although complex and highly technical in its language, the initiative was enthusiastically favored by Reagan, who never met a tax he didn't try to limit. The governor did his best, but fierce opposition by Democrats and special interest groups concerned about future funding combined to defeat the measure by a vote of 54 percent to 46 percent. Sometimes, however, you win by losing. Proposition 1 spawned a series of parallel efforts in twenty other states. With the success of Howard Jarvis's Proposition 13 in 1978 (just five years later) and the passage of similar laws in twelve other states that same year, Reagan's initiative can be seen as the birth of the tax limitation movement in America.[75]

There were some detractors of the Reagan record. A *Los Angeles Times* analyst wrote dismissively that Reagan had left footprints on the government of California that "can be swept away as easily as if he had walked on sand." But Lou Cannon, the liberal journalist who covered Ronald Reagan for nearly forty years, arrived at a far different conclusion: "Reagan set a tone of skepticism about liberal, expansionist government that persists to this day in California." From a standing start as a political novice, Reagan "mastered the intricacies of governing the nation's most populous and macroscopic state." He proved as no one had before him that it was possible "to succeed as governor of a major state without abandoning conservative principles." Furthermore, wrote Cannon, Reagan carried his doctrine of limited government "to the national political stage, from which he tugged the nation in a conservative direction."[76] And Ed Meese was with Ronald Reagan all the way, helping him to master the intricacies of governing and to perfect his unique blend of political success and philosophical principle.

Chapter III

HELPING THE CANDIDATE

~~

Between 1974 and 1980, Ronald Reagan left the governorship of California, launched a successful speaking and radio commentary career, and contested an incumbent Republican president for the 1976 presidential nomination and almost won. He then resumed his speech-making and radio commentaries and laid plans for another try at the presidency, traveling to Western Europe to strengthen his foreign policy credentials. He bested six of the GOP's best and brightest in 1980 for the party's nomination and decisively won the general election against another incumbent president who underestimated him, as had every one of his opponents since he entered politics. The supporting cast around Reagan expanded and contracted depending upon the demands of the moment. Because Ed Meese's forte was governance and public policy rather than electoral politics, he was not as visible during these years as he had been in Sacramento. But he was there when needed, participating in early strategy sessions for the 1976 attempt and finally joining the campaign staff full time, assuming a central role in the 1980 campaign, and laying the foundation for what is generally regarded by politicians and academics as the most successful presidential transition in modern politics.

In May 1974, when it was uncertain whether President Nixon would survive Watergate, Governor Reagan discussed his presidential prospects with advisers new and old at his Pacific Palisades home. Present were Meese, Lyn Nofziger, Mike Deaver, public relations specialist Peter Hannaford, "Kitchen Cabinet" members Holmes Tuttle, Justin Dart, and David Packard, and two outsiders—John Sears, a thirty-four-year-old campaign consultant from Washington, D.C., and Mississippi State Republican Chairman Clarke Reed. Reagan listened attentively as Sears predicted Nixon would not survive, Ford would not be able to run the country, and the way was open for Reagan to run for president in 1976. While many of Sears's ideas were initially rejected by the Californians, according to Lou Cannon, he helped "plant the seeds" for the Reagan challenge to President Ford—and wound up directing the challenge.[77]

But in the spring of 1974, a cautious Reagan adopted a wait-and-see attitude that was endorsed by his advisers, including Meese. In the meantime, after nearly eight years of 12-hour days serving the governor of the most populous state in the country, Ed Meese decided to try something different: he became vice president for administration of Rohr Industries, an aerospace and transportation company based in Chula Vista, just outside San Diego. He liked the company and its chairman, Burt F. Raynes, the pay was good, and there was never any snow in San Diego. Reagan sent him on his way with a hearty slap on the back, remarking, "Ed Meese deserves much of the credit for this administration's successes."[78]

But Meese soon discovered that he was not a corporate person. He had turned down the possibility of a judgeship and a full-time

partnership in a law firm for the same reason—they were too con-
fining. He was at his best when he was keeping a dozen balls in the
air at the same time. "He liked the Rohr people," recalls Ursula
Meese, "but it was not a good fit."[79] Knowing he would be happier
out on his own, Meese left Rohr in May 1976 to return to private
law practice, affiliating with Knutson, Tobin, Meyer and Shannon,
based in La Mesa outside San Diego.

His first "client" was Ronald Reagan, who was trying to wrest the
Republican presidential nomination from President Ford. Meese
had stayed in contact with Mike Deaver, Pete Hannaford, Lyn
Nofziger, and Richard Wirthlin throughout 1975 and into 1976.
They usually met over breakfast to discuss political developments
and how to answer arguments such as, "The GOP's only chance to
keep the White House in 1976 is to rally behind Ford as the incumbent." Another frequent topic was the growing number of "name"
Californians who had supported Reagan in the past but who were
now coming out for Ford. "We agreed," recalled Hannaford, "that
the tactic was transparent and would not work." In fact, the attempt
to discourage Reagan from running by suggesting that his friends
were deserting him "had the opposite effect."[80]

A key factor in Reagan's decision was President Ford's refusal
to meet with famed Russian dissident and author Alexander Sol-
zhenitsyn. Reagan made it clear that if he had been president he
would have been honored to sit down with the famed survivor and
chronicler of the Gulag Archipelago. Announcing his candidacy in
November 1975, Reagan was established as an early favorite to win
the New Hampshire primary. But he lost it, albeit narrowly, when
his overly protective campaign manager John Sears pulled him
out of the state the weekend before primary day. Ford rode New

Hampshire's momentum to win GOP primaries in Massachusetts, Vermont, Illinois (Reagan's native state), and Florida. If Reagan also lost North Carolina, almost every observer agreed, he would probably fade from national prominence like so many other promising candidates in American politics.

Drawing on inner reserves of strength and faith, Reagan went on the offensive against Ford's detentist foreign policy and its principal architect, Secretary of State Henry Kissinger. With considerable help from Senator Jesse Helms, who loaned his state organization to the Reagan campaign, and after two weeks of nonstop barnstorming in the Tarheel State, Reagan upset Ford by 53 to 46 percent. The nature of the nomination race was fundamentally altered. Like two heavyweights standing in the middle of the ring and trading their best punches, Reagan and Ford each won key primaries in the following months.

By mid-July, when Ed Meese had formally joined the Reagan campaign, the delegate count was extraordinarily close: Ford led with just under 1,100 delegates while Reagan closely trailed with 1,000. The media played up the horserace nature of the contest, but something more important was occurring—a seismic shift in American politics. Former Democrat Reagan was forging a new majority of Republicans, Democrats, and Independents under the Republican banner. A special target was the George Wallace Democrats to whom Reagan offered something to vote *for* rather than *against*. Both Reagan and outsider Democrat Jimmy Carter were doing well, wrote analyst Richard Whalen, because they were "perceived as unsullied by Watergate, untainted by Vietnam, and uncorrupted by a Washington system that isn't working."[81]

In a calculated last-minute attempt to gain uncommitted delegates,

Sears persuaded Reagan to name moderate Senator Richard Sch- weiker of Pennsylvania as his running mate. Seemingly disparate in their political philosophy, Reagan and Schweiker had much in com- mon. Both were strongly anti-abortion and shared many of the same concerns about the decline of the family and the community. Al- though the Schweiker gambit failed to move delegates into the Rea- gan column, the final roll call of delegates for the presidential nomina- tion was astonishingly close—1,187 for Ford, 1,070 for Reagan. Some conservatives criticized Reagan's selection of Schweiker as blatantly political, but Meese and other members of the governor's inner circle agreed that it kept the Republican National Convention from being "a cut-and-dried coronation" of Ford.[82]

Meese, Pete Hannaford, and Martin Anderson worked hard dur- ing meetings of the Platform Committee to ensure that the plat- form was consistent with Reagan's views and stated positions. They came up with the thematic statement "Morality in Foreign Policy" to serve as a preamble to the foreign policy section of the platform and to emphasize the difference between the *realpolitik* of Ford- Kissinger and Reagan's commitment to victory in the Cold War. It read in part: "Ours will be a foreign policy which recognizes that in international negotiations we must make no undue concessions; that in pursuing detente we must not grant unilateral favors with only the hope of getting future favors in return."[83] Soviet leader Mikhail Gorbachev would have done well to read the 1976 Repub- lican Platform before sitting down a decade later to negotiate with President Reagan.

"The Cause Goes On"

Early on the final convention day, Reagan addressed his disappointed supporters, many of them weeping, and urged them not to give up their ideals. Millions of Americans, he said, "want what you want . . . a shining city on a hill." "We lost," he acknowledged, "but the cause—the cause goes on." And then he added a couple of lines from an old English ballad, "I'll lay me down and bleed awhile; though I am wounded, I am not slain. I shall rise and fight again."[84] Reagan's recovery was rapid, helped by the electric response of the delegates, and a national television audience that evening, to a brief impromptu speech in which he outlined some of the goals he would have pursued as president. "Beautiful, just beautiful," Vice President Nelson Rockefeller was heard to say as he grasped Reagan's hand.[85]

At an early September luncheon meeting at his home in Pacific Palisades, Reagan discussed the future with Meese, Sears, Wirthlin, Hannaford, Deaver, and other advisers, including the issues he expected to raise in 1977. He spoke of the "victory" of the conservative platform adopted at Kansas City and said he would campaign for the GOP ticket that fall "without accommodating Ford on issues on which they disagreed."[86] Despite the complaints of the Ford people that Reagan did not do enough, he campaigned vigorously in twenty states for the president and other Republican candidates. And he was greeted with unusual enthusiasm wherever he went. Hotel staffs would line up to say goodbye when he checked out. Off-duty policemen would volunteer to serve as his escort. People constantly implored him: "Governor, you have to run again." Mike Deaver, who accompanied Reagan on his travels that fall, told Peter Hannaford: "There's something remarkable going on out there."[87]

Following Ford's disappointing loss to Carter, Ronald Reagan began preparing to run again for the presidency. He formed a political action committee, Citizens for the Republic, financed by $1 million left over from his try for the Republican presidential nomination. A Gallup Poll found that he was known by nine of ten Americans and was their first choice to be the GOP's 1980 nominee. In a three-hour meeting with national security expert Richard V. Allen, he outlined his view of the Cold War, based on a simple proposition: "We win and they lose."[88] He burnished his foreign policy credentials with trips to London, Berlin, and Paris, where he met political leaders such as Margaret Thatcher and Helmut Kohl. He approved Martin Anderson's plan to form a national network of issue task forces. By Election Day 1980, the Reagan campaign had signed up 461 experts for forty-eight different task forces, including such policy heavyweights as Milton Friedman, Alan Greenspan, George Shultz, and Jeane Kirkpatrick.

In March 1979, Senator Paul Laxalt of Nevada announced the formation of the "exploratory" Reagan for President Committee. Three years earlier, Laxalt had been a lonely Washington voice for Reagan—one of only two members of Congress to support the former California governor. This time, he was joined by a dozen senators and representatives and over 365 prominent Republicans as founding members of the committee, including former Treasury Secretary William Simon and former Health, Education and Welfare Secretary Caspar Weinberger. The campaign staff closely resembled the 1976 team: Paul Laxalt, national chairman; John Sears, director of day-to-day operations; Mike Deaver, political tactician and chief fundraiser; Lyn Nofziger, press secretary; Richard Wirthlin, director of polling; Martin Anderson, domestic policy coordinator; and Richard Allen, foreign policy coordinator.

Helping but not yet full-time was Ed Meese because he was still teaching at the University of San Diego Law School, running the Center for Criminal Justice Policy and Management there, and practicing law. After leaving Rohr and returning to private law practice, Meese had reflected upon his experience as a deputy district attorney and chief of staff to Governor Reagan. It seemed to him that over the past several decades criminal justice in America had been turned around so that the rights of the criminals too often took precedence over the rights of the victims. The scales of justice were increasingly tilted in the courtroom in favor of the defense rather than the prosecution. Redress was urgently needed. He believed he could help reverse this disturbing trend in law enforcement through research and education.

With a grant from the Sarah Scaife Foundation, recalls Meese, "I developed a plan for a law school center for criminal justice policy and management." It was envisioned that the center would provide research "not slanted toward the defense of criminals" but to include the perspective of law enforcement and the prosecution. It would study the different aspects of criminal law and procedure, including the impact of the Supreme Court's *Miranda* ruling on the ability of police to function and victims' rights such as the right to appear before a judge prior to sentencing. The University of San Diego, a private Catholic school, approved the proposal, and from the fall of 1977 through January 1981, Ed Meese served as professor of law at USD and director of the Center for Criminal Justice Policy and Management, while continuing to practice law.

The Center assisted victims in obtaining legal representation, provided research and consultation to attorneys involved in victims' rights cases, and helped legislators and legislative committees in the drafting of statutes dealing with victim compensation laws. The Center published several studies with Americans for Effective Law Enforcement, run by Frank Carrington, often called "the founder of the victims of crime movement."[89] Among Carrington's seminal works was *Neither Cruel Nor Unusual: The Case for Capital Punishment*, published in 1978. During this same period, Meese served as vice chairman of California's Organized Crime Control Commission and was active in the criminal law section of the California Bar Association.

USD professor Richard Huffman attended the Center's programs and was impressed with its "systemic approach" to criminal justice. Now an associate justice of California's Court of Appeals in San Diego, Judge Huffman says that the Center under Ed Meese generated "valuable research" and made a "worthwhile contribution" to the discussion of the criminal justice/sentencing process. What impressed Huffman was Meese's academic approach. "Actually," Huffman says, "Ed Meese is a scholar. He wanted to foster debate and he enjoyed engaging in scholarly debate. He was not an ideologue."[90]

In November 1979, when Reagan formally became a candidate for the Republican presidential nomination, Ed Meese went from part to almost full-time in the campaign, and found himself in the middle of a fierce struggle for power between John Sears and nearly everyone else. Unwilling to share authority (particularly with Californians close to Reagan) and convinced that Reagan needed him and his political expertise more than anyone else, Sears maneuvered the dismissal of Lyn Nofziger; deliberately alienated Martin Anderson by setting up a parallel policy development operation in Washington, D.C.; and told Reagan he had to choose between him and Mike Deaver. Knowing how much Reagan disliked making personnel decisions, and for the good of the campaign, Deaver resigned, over Reagan's protest.

Meese bluntly told Reagan he had made "a serious mistake" in letting Deaver go and even suggested, according to Lou Cannon, that the candidate didn't understand what was happening in his campaign.[91] In truth, because of his success over the years as a negotiator, Reagan believed he could reconcile any serious differences among the leadership of his team. But Sears made that impossible. Far from being upset by his bluntness, Meese remembers, "the governor and Nancy asked me to take a greater role."[92] He agreed, promising to come aboard full-time in January, and making himself the next target for the political insider from the East who thought he was irreplaceable.

Leaving the Rose Garden

When Sears began pressing Reagan to get rid of Meese for supposed incompetence—some position papers had allegedly not been produced on time—and suggested Bill Clark, his former chief of staff, as Meese's replacement, Reagan had enough. Confronting Sears, he said: "You got Deaver, but by God, you're not going to get Ed Meese!" In truth, Reagan and Sears had never connected. "He never looks me in the eye," complained Reagan, "he looks me in the tie." Reagan's decision to fire Sears was compounded by his unexpected if narrow loss to George H.W. Bush in the Iowa caucuses—after following an above the fray strategy laid down by Sears. Lyn Nofziger pointedly commented: "If you're going to follow a Rose

Garden strategy, you better be sure you have a Rose Garden."[93]

Poor morale and constant bickering were not the only problems created by Sears. As Reagan pointed out in his autobiography, the campaign had been spending so furiously—some $13 million of the primary allowance of $17 million had been expended or committed by Iowa—that "we were in danger of exceeding limits established by federal election laws." Demonstrating he could fire and hire when he had to, Reagan decided to make the change at the top before the New Hampshire results were in. "If I lost and then fired Sears," wrote Reagan, "people could say I was trying to make him the scapegoat for my loss, and I didn't want that to happen."[94]

But Reagan was determined to win in New Hampshire. He barnstormed all over the Granite State by bus for almost three weeks and debated Bush not once but twice, besting him both times. Gerald Carmen, the former chairman of the state Republican Party, built a network of Reagan volunteers, including members of single-issue groups like right-to-life and anti-gun control groups, and directed it from a crowded, chaotic office in downtown Manchester. Liberal columnist Mark Shields, contrasting Carmen's working-class background with the upscale past of Bush manager Susan McLane, suggested that the race was "between Schlitz and sherry, between citizenship papers and collected papers, between night school and graduate school."[95]

In the early afternoon of primary day, Reagan called in John Sears and his assistants and asked them to resign—which they did—and then named as his new campaign director Wall Streeter William J. Casey, who had been doing some consulting for the campaign. Ed Meese became chief of staff in charge of day-to-day campaign operations. Reagan took Richard Wirthlin aside and said to him,

"Dick, I'd like you to be in charge of strategy from here on out."[96] In a sense, the campaign triumvirate of Casey, Meese, and Wirthlin anticipated the White House troika of Reagan's first presidential term. Furthermore, and in short order, Mike Deaver, Lyn Nofziger, and Martin Anderson rejoined the Reagan campaign. Those who knew what Ronald Reagan wanted and were committed to his agenda, not their own, were back. "The key to a Reagan victory," Mike Deaver later wrote, "would not be found around a green velvet table in a smoke-filled room; it would be found at the campaign rally and the debate lectern and in the television studio where Reagan could look voters in the eye and tell them why he's the right man for the job."[97] Aided by Verne Orr, the former California state finance director whom Meese had installed in the Los Angeles office, Bill Casey quickly restored the campaign to fiscal solvency.

The political momentum shifted sharply. Howard Baker, John Connally, Bob Dole, Phil Crane, and John Anderson soon withdrew from the Republican nomination race. Reagan kept beating Bush in primary after primary until in late May, Bush at last conceded the 1980 Republican nomination to Reagan. Bush's decision was realistic and politic: he was widely mentioned as a possible running mate for Reagan.

When CBS's Mike Wallace asked Reagan in a television interview whether it wasn't "arrogant" of him to want to take over the direction of "the greatest superpower in the world," the candidate replied calmly, "I find myself very conscious of the size and difficulty of the undertaking." But bear in mind, he added, that in seeking the office he was not being politically ambitious. A skeptical Wallace asked Reagan to explain what he meant. "I'm not on any ego trip or glory ride," Reagan said. "I'm running because I think there is a job to do and I want to do it."[98]

But first he had to beat the incumbent President Jimmy Carter. And some Republicans thought the best way to accomplish that was with a "dream ticket" of Ronald Reagan and Gerald Ford. The possibility was reinforced by an unexpectedly dynamic speech on the opening night of the Republican National Convention in Detroit by former President Ford, who declared, "This country means too much to me to comfortably sit on the park bench. So, when this convention fields the team for Governor Reagan, count me in."[99] In fact, the Reagan campaign had been seriously considering vice presidential possibilities since the spring. Dick Wirthlin had conducted lengthy in-home surveys of twenty potential running mates. Edward Schmults, a well-known New York lawyer and alumnus of the Treasury Department, had carefully vetted a dozen of the top-tier vice presidential candidates. A small group of five—Ronald and Nancy Reagan, Bill Casey, Dick Wirthlin and Ed Meese—had carefully and privately considered the findings. Ford was at the top of the list, followed by George Bush. Choosing Ford, Wirthlin later wrote, "would have sent a strong signal to moderate voters."[100]

So it was that in Detroit the two political leaders asked their aides to see if they could arrive at a compromise regarding the shared duties and responsibilities of a future president and a past president. Representing Reagan were Ed Meese, Bill Casey and Dick Wirthlin; the Ford people were Henry Kissinger, Alan Greenspan, Jack Marsh, and Robert Barrett. The two groups met several times over the next two days amid increasing skepticism on the Reagan side. Among the conditions proposed by those negotiating for Ford was that the White House staff would report to President Reagan through Vice President Ford. Ford also wanted to pick the

secretary of state and the secretary of defense although he gener-
ously offered Reagan a veto. But in turn Ford wanted veto rights
on Reagan's cabinet selections. Easily perceived in all of this was
Kissinger's Metternichian hand. When Meese showed the long list
of Ford's demands to Lyn Nofziger, the ever blunt Nofziger said,
"He wants us to give away the store." "Exactly," Meese replied, "but
we're not going to do it."[101]

The dying of the dream ticket came quickly and publicly. Appearing on CBS, Ford admitted he was considering the vice presidency.
Walter Cronkite asked Ford directly, "It's got to be something like
a co-presidency?" Although "co-presidency" was not his word, Ford
did not reject it, replying, "That's something Governor Reagan really ought to consider." Reagan was dismayed: No one had suggested
there ought to be two presidents in the White House. While their
aides continued trying to square a circle, Ford and Reagan sepa-
rately decided at almost the same moment that it wouldn't work.
Meeting in Reagan's suite on nomination night, the once and future
presidents talked quietly for about ten minutes about the campaign
they might have run together. "He was a gentleman," Reagan said
afterward about Ford. "I feel we're friends now."[102]

Eager to assert his command of the convention, Reagan telephoned a surprised George Bush and offered him second place on
his ticket. An elated Bush responded, "I can campaign enthusiastically for your election and your platform." When reporters brought
up Bush's characterization of Reagan's supply-side theory of economics as "voodoo economics," Meese quipped, "Well, he had his
exorcism in Detroit."[103]

"Are You Better Off?"

After the convention, the Reagan for President headquarters were moved from near the Los Angeles airport to Arlington, Virginia, where Ed Meese shared an apartment with Drew Lewis, liaison with the Republican National Committee and a skilled political operative. Even for the seemingly tireless Meese, the days were long. He would breakfast with Bill Casey in Casey's apartment at 6:30 a.m., discussing the day's agenda and what had happened or not happened the day before, and arrive at Reagan headquarters at 7:30 a.m. He would spend the rest of the day and much of the evening coordinating, along with Casey, Lewis, political director William Timmons, and veteran politician F. Clifton White, the myriad details of a presidential campaign, including the care and feeding of the candidate; communications internal and external; the distribution of buttons, bumper stickers, and other materials; relations with Republican state chairmen, national committeemen and committeewomen; liaison with Republican candidates seeking reelection as well as those challenging Democratic incumbents; campaign spending (there were new rules and regulations because 1980 was the first presidential election to be federally funded); and, most important of all, getting out all the vote on Election Day. With Reagan on the campaign plane were policy experts Martin Anderson and Dick Allen, personal aide Deaver, press secretary Nofziger, and the acerbic but astute political tactician Stuart Spencer, who had helped guide Reagan to his 1966 gubernatorial victory.

Meese had another responsibility which only a few at the very top were aware of—planning the transition to a Reagan administration, with an emphasis on staffing. In April 1980, Pendleton James approached his old friend Ed Meese—he had known both Ed and Ursula before they were married—and said he wanted to help Reagan in any way he could. Meese asked James, who had worked in President Nixon's personnel office, "to start thinking about the transition in case they won the election." Using primary campaign funds, he set James up in a small office in Los Angeles separate from the campaign headquarters.[104] When Bill Casey became campaign director, he tried to shut down James's operation, concerned that if knowledge of it leaked, Reagan would appear arrogant about his chances of being nominated and elected.

But Meese had been told by Martin Anderson, among others, what a "shambles" the Nixon transition had been. Convinced that careful advance planning was the key to a successful transition, he set up a meeting among Reagan, Casey, James, and himself to decide the fate of the transition effort. Casey argued that it was too risky, James recalls. Word of what they were doing was sure to leak and would hurt Reagan. Meese countered that transition planning was too important to be shut down. "Pen," asked Reagan, "can you do this without it leaking out?" "Certainly, I can," replied James. "Then I agree with Ed," said Reagan. "Go ahead." Rather than accepting the advice of his campaign director, Reagan sided with Meese, trusting his judgment and foresight. "Ed had an uncanny ability to look down the road," says James.[105]

When the Reagan headquarters was relocated to northern Virginia in September, the transition office followed but was again set up in a different location, in Alexandria. "I used to meet with Pen, Helene von Damm, and others, sometimes for breakfast at 6:30 a.m. but more regularly at their office from 10 or 11 to midnight," remembers Meese.[106] He noted approvingly that the Reagan transition team was covering all the bases, getting in touch with people who had been with Nixon and Ford and who were associated with think tanks such as The Heritage Foundation, the American Enterprise Institute, and the Hoover Institution, all of which were preparing studies about the possible policies of a Reagan administration. Meese himself met with Charles Heatherly, the editor of Heritage's mammoth 1,000-page study, *Mandate for Leadership: Policy Management in a Conservative Administration.* On one occasion, Meese gave a pep talk to the editors of the Heritage study, whose only compensation for their many hours of volunteer work in the evenings and on the weekends was pizza and beer.

The Reagan transition team applied a set of five criteria to the initial list of candidates to determine who would be included in the short list for top administrative positions: commitment to Ronald Reagan's political philosophy, integrity, toughness, competence, and being a team player. "If you [were] coming in to serve in this administration," James explained later, "you [had to] know what Reagan ran on."[107]

Although all the national polls placed Reagan well ahead of President Carter immediately following the Republican convention in July, the president got a sizable bump from the Democratic convention and some rhetorical mistakes by Reagan, such as his suggestion—at a national rally of evangelical Christians—that "creationism" ought to be taught in public schools as an alternative to Darwin's theory of evolution. By Labor Day, the candidates were about even. But as Lou Cannon put it, Carter was dogged by "the captivity of hostages he could not free, an economy he could not improve, and an opponent he could not shake."[108]

Reagan set about courting the blue-collar, ethnic, Catholic vote, concentrating on Carter's sorry economic record—the nation was being strangled by "stagflation," double-digit inflation coupled with zero economic growth—and endeavoring to reassure the voters that he could handle the weighty duties of the presidency. "Our message, to traditional Democrats, " explained Ed Meese, "was that the Republican party of traditional values and economic growth offered them a better prospect of effective government than did the crumbling New Deal coalition."[109] When Carter refused to participate in a three-way debate with Reagan and Independent John Anderson, Reagan readily agreed to appear with the Republican Congressman turned Independent. Although one poll said that viewers believed Anderson had "outplayed" Reagan, a *New York Times*/CBS poll suggested that Reagan was the true beneficiary because a greater number of people believed that the former California governor understood the complicated problems facing a president, had a clear position on the issues, offered a clear vision of where he wanted to lead the country, and would exercise good judgment under pressure. The poll said that Reagan now led Carter by five points.

With two weeks left in the campaign, Reagan held a lead of about seven points in the popular vote and a comfortable margin in the electoral vote. But the Reagan organization was concerned about one issue over which it had no control—the fifty-two American hostages in Tehran. If they were freed at the eleventh hour, how would the public react? Would the American people be caught up in the euphoria of the moment and reelect Carter? Or would they dismiss the release as October politics and vote their pocketbooks? Reagan and his top advisers met in New York City, following the candidate's effective appearance at the annual Alfred E. Smith Memorial Dinner, to decide whether to sit on a safe but slim lead or play their last card—a televised debate with Jimmy Carter.

Bill Timmons thought the debate was too high a risk and talked about the superior Republican organization that would turn out the vote on Election Day. Dick Wirthlin said Reagan was ahead by almost seven points—why take a chance on losing a solid lead by debating a trailing candidate? Stu Spencer, who had been suggesting a debate to Reagan for some time, argued it would serve as a "hedge" against any October surprise, such as the release of the hostages. He also said that a debate would "freeze" the candidates where they were—with Reagan in the lead. Deaver, Casey, and Nofziger all favored the debate. Houston lawyer James Baker, who had joined the Reagan organization as a "senior adviser" after managing George Bush's unsuccessful campaign against Reagan, said that Reagan had to debate or risk defeat. Meese played "his usual collegial role," ensuring that the dissenting views of Wirthlin and Timmons were heard, but he too favored the debate.[110] Reagan followed the advice of his political strategists and his own political instincts and agreed to meet Carter for the highest stakes in American politics—the presidency.

On the evening of October 28, one week before Election Day, the two candidates stood behind specially constructed podiums on the stage of Cleveland's Music Hall. The audience was an estimated 105 million Americans. Carter was tight-lipped and rarely looked at his opponent. He immediately went on the attack and stayed there for ninety minutes, constantly describing Reagan's ideas and positions as "dangerous," "disturbing," and "radical."[111] Reagan was calm, cool, smiling. He patiently explained where Carter had misquoted or misrepresented him, much like a professor gently pointing out the errors of a poorly prepared student.

The climax of the debate and the effective end of the campaign came when Carter tried to link Reagan with the idea of making Social Security voluntary and argued that Reagan had opposed Medicare. (Reagan had in fact supported an alternative sponsored by the American Medical Association.) That familiar crooked grin appeared on Reagan's face, and with a rueful shake of his head, he looked at Carter and said, "There you go again." The Carter campaign of fear collapsed in an instant. In his closing remarks, Reagan looked straight into the camera and quietly asked the viewer, "Are you better off than you were four years ago?"[112] An Associated Press poll found that 46 percent of those watching thought Reagan did the better job, with 34 percent saying Carter did. Another survey showed that undecided voters were moving toward Reagan by a two-to-one margin.

Although most of the national polls said it would be a close election, Reagan won by an electoral landslide and more than eight million in the popular vote. He carried forty-four states (the same number as Lyndon Johnson in his 1964 runaway victory over Barry Goldwater) and amassed 489 electoral votes. His total of 43.9 million votes was the second highest on record, behind only Richard Nixon's 47.2 million in 1972. His political coattails helped the GOP to pick up twelve seats in the Senate, giving it majority control for the first time in a quarter of a century. In the House, Republicans registered a gain of 33 seats, almost all of them conservatives. *The Washington Post* called the Reagan victory a "tidal wave." Pollster Lou Harris (John Kennedy's favorite) described it as "stunning." Former Democratic presidential candidate George McGovern said the voters had "abandoned American liberalism."[113]

The "Most Effective" Transition

When President-elect Reagan formally appointed Ed Meese director of the transition, Meese was more than ready: He and Pen James had been preparing for the assignment for seven months. The result was what two knowledgeable political scientists called "the most carefully planned and effective [transition] in American political history."[114] Even with all the advance planning, it was a massive undertaking. More than 1,000 people worked on the transition—311 received federal funds, another 331 served for a token $1, and the reminder were volunteers. Despite inflation, the Reagan transition spent less of the taxpayers' money than the Carter team had four years earlier, $1.75 million versus $1.78 million.

The largest component of the transition was the Executive Branch Management division, headed by Bill Timmons, who had served as Reagan's political director and had worked previously in the White House and the Washington political community. Timmons sent teams into seventy-three departments and government agencies to survey their activities and prepare a detailed briefing for the new appointees. Nothing was overlooked. The briefing books included where the office was located, how many people worked there, what government programs were involved, which congressmen and senators had oversight responsibilities for the programs, a detailed list of major decisions to make within the first weeks (or even days) after taking office in January, and any pending legal problems. Timmons's reports, commented Martin Anderson, were the kind of "detailed dossier" that might be put together about a large company being considered for purchase.[115]

Pen James headed the second group, which dealt with presidential appointments. The incoming members of the cabinet were informed they could not choose the people who would work for them without clearing their names with the president-elect or his top personal aides. All key sub-cabinet appointments were treated as presidential appointments even when they were not. It was emphasized that, with few exceptions, all incumbent political appointees should be dismissed. "We made sure," Ed Meese said, "that we cleaned out all the appointees of the past administration. We felt an empty office was better than to have a holdover."[116]

To keep track of all the policy planning and research (building on the work of the hundreds of policy analysts who had worked during the campaign), Meese named Darrell Trent director of the Office of Policy Coordination. Trent had served as Martin Anderson's deputy during the campaign, overseeing domestic policy analysis at the headquarters while Anderson was with candidate Reagan on the campaign plane. The transition effort, Meese wrote, was "aided greatly" by a yearlong research project of The Heritage Foundation—*Mandate for Leadership*.

On Thursday evening, November 6, 1980, just two days after Reagan was elected the Fortieth President of the United States, Edwin J. Feulner, Phillip N. Truluck, and Charles Heatherly of Heritage personally delivered manuscript copies of *Mandate* (each numbering twenty volumes and weighing thirty pounds) to Ed Meese, Martin Anderson, and Richard Allen, Reagan's national security adviser. The six men met in a private dining room in the lower lobby of the Hay-Adams Hotel, opposite the White House. Having visited with Heatherly and other editors, Meese had a good idea of what was coming, but none of the Reagan aides was prepared for the magnitude of *Mandate*.

Even Meese did not expect to receive more than 2,000 specific recommendations to move the federal government in a conservative direction, including boosting the defense budget by $20 billion in fiscal year 1981 and increasing it by an average of $35 billion over the next five years; establishing urban "enterprise zones" to breathe new life into the nation's cities; reducing personal income tax rates by 10 percent across the board; calling for line item veto power by the President; and developing a new strategic bomber by using B-1 and advanced bomber technology. President Reagan liked Heritage's ideas so much he suggested that *Mandate* be given to every cabinet officer at the very first cabinet meeting. "Place a copy on the seat of each Cabinet member's chair," Meese instructed his assistant Kenneth Cribb, "so they will have to pick it up and read it."[117]

A key part of the transition process was the "strategic outline of initial actions" prepared by Dick Wirthlin and to be implemented during the first 180 days of the Administration, from the inauguration to early August when Congress usually recessed for a summer vacation. The outline drew in large part on an address Reagan had delivered in September 1980 when he proposed strictly controlling the rate of government spending, reducing personal income tax rates, revising government regulations, establishing a stable monetary policy, and following a consistent national economic policy. Anderson and the other economists were confident that Reagan could cut taxes, balance the budget, and increase domestic growth given the right kind of cooperation by Congress. *The Wall Street Journal* agreed, commenting that Reagan had "spelled out a prudent, gradual, responsible reordering of economic priorities."[118]

Observers Left and Right praised the Reagan transition as superbly conceived and implemented—another example of Ed Meese's ability to do an important job well. And yet when President-elect Reagan selected his chief of staff, he bypassed Meese, who nearly everyone assumed had a lock on the job, and instead picked Jim Baker. Baker's most important campaign contribution had been to help prepare Reagan for the television debate with Jimmy Carter.

Widely varying reasons have been suggested as to why Reagan named Baker rather than Meese to be his chief aide, such as Meese's alleged disorganization (the "bottomless briefcase" canard) and lack of Washington experience; long-standing antipathy toward Meese on the part of Stu Spencer, who favored Baker as did Mike Deaver; Nancy Reagan's alleged distaste for Meese's mode of dress and even his weight; Meese's supposed inability to "swap Eurochat" with Pamela Harriman, the reigning Georgetown hostess, (according to authorized Reagan biographer Edmund Morris).

In his autobiography, Reagan offers no explanation, but a reasonable one may be arrived at once you realize that three men—Ed Meese, Jim Baker, and Mike Deaver—were involved in the president-elect's decision. He wished all three to serve in the White House and to the best of their respective abilities—Baker as the shrewd political operative who knew how Washington worked; Meese as the "conceptualizer" who could translate Reagan's ideas into policies and programs better than anyone else; and Deaver as the director of what he called "presidential stagecraft"—framing effectively Reagan's public events. Reagan had been well served by the triumvirate of Casey, Meese, and Wirthlin during the presidential campaign. He had read about Nixon's White House team of Robert Haldeman, John Erlichman, and Henry Kissinger. The creation of the Baker-Meese-Deaver troika proved that Reagan could make difficult and even painful decisions about personnel when required.

Reagan knew that Meese would be upset and even hurt at not getting the top staff position. When he offered the chief of staff post to Baker, he remarked that Meese had been very valuable to him through the years, and he hoped that Baker "would be able to work" with him. Baker replied that he was confident he could and suggested that Meese be given the title of Counsellor to the President with "Cabinet rank." Reagan thought Baker's suggestion was "a fine idea."[119]

When Meese and Deaver met later with the president-elect, Reagan told Meese that he would not be getting the top spot but would share responsibility for running the White House with Baker. Meese seemed stunned and later told Deaver he was not certain he could accept a "secondary" position.[120] But once his sharp disappointment had ebbed and he had talked with Ursula, Ed Meese decided he had been a loyal member of the Reagan team too long to quit now. He remembered one of Reagan's favorite sayings: "There's no limit to what a man can do or where he can go, if he doesn't mind who gets the credit."[121] Ed Meese's willingness to become a member of the White House troika may have been the most selfless act of his career.

Using a piece of standard typing paper and bureaucratic shorthand, Baker and Meese divided up their duties at a November 17, 1980, meeting. The one-page memorandum listed Meese's as: "Counsellor to the President for Policy (with cabinet rank); member Super Cabinet Executive Committee (in absence of The President and V-P preside over meetings); participate as a principal in all meetings of full Cabinet; coordination and supervision of responsibilities of The Secretary to the Cabinet; coordination and supervision of work of the Domestic Policy Studies and the National Security Council; with Baker coordination and supervision of work of OMB, CEA, CEQ, Trade Rep and S&T; participation as a principal in all policy group meetings; attend any meeting which Pres attends — w/ his consent."[122] It was an impressive catalog of responsibilities.

For his part, Baker gave up a seat in the Cabinet and the large corner office in the West Wing that had been Henry Kissinger's to Meese, but secured control over every document intended for the President's eyes as well as all presidential appointments and the President's schedule. In practical terms, Meese would not be able to get the President to hire anyone or sign anything "unless he persuaded the Chief [of Staff] first."[123]

Disagreements and disputes were inevitable, along with the usual bureaucratic infighting by staff assistants, but if the record of the first four Reagan years is fairly judged, the troika worked well for the President, the country, and the world. That is certainly the judgment of its three members. "Notwithstanding the tensions and that we were sometimes on different sides of an issue," says Jim Baker, "history will attest to the success of the troika." When it came to "getting things done for the President," like the Economic Recovery Tax Act, "we got them done. We operated [on the ERTA] with laser-like efficiency." And, adds Baker, "we didn't have any Iran-Contras." It was a perfect but bumpy arrangement," says Mike Deaver. "Ronald Reagan was well served." Meese concurs, describing the troika with its allocation of responsibilities as "a very good thing for the President."[124]

But first Ed Meese had a job to do as director of the transition,

starting with cabinet selections. A group of about twenty, including members of the California "kitchen cabinet" and those who had
held leadership positions in the presidential campaign, were asked
to suggest a dozen or more candidates for each cabinet position.
Wealthy businessman Jack Wrather, a personal friend of Reagan
from his Hollywood years, remembered vividly a "brilliant briefing"
that Meese conducted for him and other kitchen cabinet members
just prior to the election. "We got lists of every single job in every
department and . . . the significance of the job . . . . I've known Ed for
a long time and had a lot of respect for him," Wrather said, but in
his analysis of the whole process he did "a monumental job."[125]

Former President Nixon had suggested Alexander Haig, former
head of NATO and his chief of staff during his last year in office,
for secretary of state. While Haig's record was impressive, Reagan
did not want somebody who would use the post as a jumping-off
point for running for president (Haig had once talked to Reagan
about possibly seeking the presidency). Meese and another transition leader met with Haig and had "a full and frank discussion" of his
plans. "We were satisfied," Meese later commented, "that he didn't
have another agenda—at least at that time." When Haig insisted
and Reagan agreed that Haig would be *the* foreign policy spokesman
for the U.S. government, he accepted the position.[126]

Caspar Weinberger's first choice had been secretary of state.
When Haig was nominated, Weinberger, Meese's colleague in Governor Reagan's cabinet, accepted secretary of defense. Bill Casey,
who also had been interested in State, informed Meese he would
still accept a place in the cabinet. From the start, Reagan wanted
Casey to be the director of the Central Intelligence Agency, a good
fit of man and mission (Casey had served in the Office of Strategic

Services during World War II). When Meese suggested elevating the job to cabinet rank, Reagan agreed.[127] For secretary of the treasury, the transition team initially considered William Simon, who had been Nixon's treasury secretary, as well as Walter Wriston, the New York banker. They settled on Donald Regan, the chairman of Merrill Lynch, after Meese came away impressed after a luncheon meeting and proposed him for the job. Many people were involved in the selection process of the Reagan cabinet but first among equals—"President-elect Reagan's top interim executive," in the words of *The Washington Post*—was Ed Meese.[128]

It therefore behooved "all students of political zoology," suggested the *Post*, to determine why the new president placed so much confidence and responsibility in a forty-nine-year-old former deputy district attorney from Alameda County. To begin with, the *Post* wrote, Meese "can be trusted to report objectively on staff recommendations." He was "loyal, does not grab for glory, create turmoil or cry wolf." He had "a quick intelligence," able to grasp complicated situations. He was "a relaxing force" who, by all available accounts, never lost his temper.

He used what he called a "college football coach" system of management, making the best use possible of the available personnel. He was fascinated by the organizational problems of constantly changing situations such as a political campaign or administration. He filled yellow legal pads with his careful notes on the myriad meetings he attended. He used colored pens to code complicated schedules and colored folders to code different subjects.

Like his boss, Meese was six feet tall and well-groomed, prone to pin stripe suits and muted ties, and had a smile that was "cherubic" and "disarming"—surprising in someone reputed to be an organization machine. "My wife says I need management charts for bedtime reading," Meese said, smiling. "That's not really true, but studying management is sort of a hobby of mine."[129]

Throughout the seventy days of the transition, Meese rose early as he always did—at 5:40 a.m.—and held his first meeting in his office at 7. He conducted interviews and briefings for the rest of the day, often skipped lunch, had a late afternoon conference call with the president-elect in California, met at 6 p.m. with his own staff, and then took a last look at the mail. Even his weekends were full: He often appeared on Sunday morning interview programs such as NBC's *Meet the Press* and CBS's *Face the Nation.* "Such a routine is not unknown in Washington," acknowledged the *Post,* "but an attending atmosphere of calm is somewhat rarer." "Ulcers?" Meese asked the reporter, laughing. "Oh, I don't think I've got ulcers, no. I've always been able to work without internalizing the pressures." "It may take Washington a little while," said a perceptive colleague, "to get used to Mr. Meese."[130] Some Washingtonians never did.

Chapter IV

COUNSELING THE PRESIDENT

~~

Two highly visible events in the first nine months of the Reagan Administration alerted the nation and the world that here was a far different kind of president. They were the passage of the Economic Recovery Tax Act and the firm handling of the strike of the air traffic controllers. A third, highly confidential event was as consequential—a small White House meeting about missile defense. Ed Meese was a major participant in all of them.

Ronald Reagan had been talking about the necessity of tax reform for decades. In 1981, the top marginal rate on individual income was 70 percent, and it stifled individual initiative and, therefore, national growth. The President argued that if you reduced tax rates and allowed people to spend or save more of what they earned, "they'll be more industrious, they'll have more incentive to work hard, and money they earn will add fuel to the great economic machine that energizes our national progress." Some economists called this approach, "supply-side economics." "I call it common sense," Reagan said.[131]

It took fireside chats with the American people, deals with

The White House

Counsellor to the President Edwin Meese and President Reagan's
first Cabinet, 1981.

moderate "boll-weevil" Democrats in the House of Representatives,
pep talks with exhausted aides, and recovery from an attempted
assassination, but on August 17, 1981, President Reagan signed the
Economic Recovery Tax Act (ERTA) into law. *Newsweek* called
it a "second New Deal potentially as profound in its import as the
first was a half century ago." The measure cut all income tax rates
by 25 percent over the next two years. It reduced the top income
tax rate from 70 percent to 50 percent, indexed tax rates to offset
the impact of inflation, and increased the tax exemption on estates
and gifts. Reagan's tax policies would fuel ninety-two months of
uninterrupted economic growth—the longest economic expansion
in peacetime to that point.

"The personal leadership of the President," Meese later wrote, "was indispensable to the program's success." When the effort was started, concerns about lost revenue dominated Hill discussions—among House Democrats headed by Speaker Tip O'Neill and Senate Republicans led by Bob Dole and Peter Domenici. But when prophecies of defeat were brought to the White House by the legislative team or by Senate Majority Leader Howard Baker, the President always gave the same answer: "Do what is necessary to get the program adopted. Don't back off. Find out what needs doing and do it. Period." In addition to exercising his unquestioned communications skills, the President exhibited the needed political will to secure the passage of tax reform. Working through his aides and directly with Congress, said Meese, Ronald Reagan demonstrated that "behind the pleasant demeanor there was a tough and determined man."[132]

As central as ERTA was to the Reagan Administration, it was only one of the dozens of policies that Meese helped coordinate. From the President's point of view, Meese was "a wonder," tackling fifty projects a day and finishing forty of them. But those who could not get Meese's attention because he was committed elsewhere had a different and critical opinion. Martin Anderson, who had previously served in the Nixon White House and had studied policymaking for two decades, thought he knew how to take full advantage of Meese's "tremendous abilities." He suggested his colleague set aside at least thirty minutes every morning to meet with the White House staff directly responsible for economic, foreign/ defense, and budget policy. Meese readily agreed, and so every day after the troika meeting of Baker, Meese, and Deaver and the daily White House staff meeting, a small group—including Anderson, national security adviser Richard Allen, Edwin Harper, the deputy director of OMB, and George Keyworth, the President's science adviser—gathered in Meese's corner office on the first floor of the West Wing. "Everything" from monetary policy to the Strategic Defense Initiative to welfare reform was discussed. The morning policy meeting in Meese's office became, Anderson said, "a critical chokepoint for the making of all policy during the early years of the Reagan administration."[133]

Lyn Nofziger, who served as White House political director during Reagan's first year, suggests that as a result of Ed Meese's so-called bottomless briefcase, "a lot of unnecessary stuff never got done. We were better off because of Ed's briefcase." But he concedes that Meese tried to do too much. "It's a good thing Ed wasn't a girl," he jokes, "because he can't say no if you need a favor."[134]

One of the most significant of the President's decisions, although not fully appreciated at the time, was the August 1981 strike of the air traffic controllers. As Ed Meese wrote in his memoir, Americans had become accustomed to public sector union walkouts. Although illegal, these strikes had usually elicited little criticism, let alone counteraction by elected officials. Any move by the Reagan Administration against the Professional Air Traffic Controllers Organization (PATCO) seemed unlikely since the organization was crucial to the functioning of the nation's aviation, and PATCO had been one of the few unions to endorse Reagan in 1980.

But the President never hesitated. During meetings with Secretary of Transportation Drew Lewis and Ed Meese, Reagan made it clear that he expected the law to be enforced. Reagan never liked to dismiss anyone, but he gave the air traffic controllers forty-eight hours to go back to work, or else. Many refused, and

The White House

President Reagan shares a laugh with Ed Meese on Meese's 50th birthday,
December 1981.

they were promptly fired and replaced. When Lewis and Meese
met in the White House on the crucial day before sanctions began,
Meese later wrote, "no one doubted the commitment and support
of the President." After Reagan's action, few public workers considered striking because everyone understood that the law would
be enforced. The firing also had "a sobering effect" on Soviet leaders who saw Reagan as a President who had to be taken seriously.
The PATCO strike, said Sovietologist Richard Pipes, showed the
Soviets "a man who, when aroused, will go to the limit to back up
his principles."[135]

In the early fall of 1981, kitchen cabinet member Jacquelin Hume
and defense specialist Karl Bendetsen spoke with Ed Meese about a
missile defense system, a long-standing objective of President Reagan, who for years had been unhappy with America's reliance on
the strategic policy of Mutual Assured Destruction (MAD). Meese
also knew about the work of The Heritage Foundation and High
Frontier, headed by former Lt. Gen. Daniel Graham, on a multi-
satellite global ballistic missile defense system. At about the same
time, Meese's former Rohr Industries boss Burt F. Raynes visited
Meese and said he had figured out that the Soviet Union was cheat-
ing on the ABM (Anti-Ballistic Missile) Treaty. At a morning policy meeting, Meese, Anderson and Dick Allen decided to bring together a select group to discuss missile defense. And so on Monday,
September 14, 1981, Ed Meese chaired the first White House discussion of what would develop into what President Reagan called
his Strategic Defense Initiative (SDI) and his critics "Star Wars."

Present, in addition to Meese, were Bendetsen, General Graham,
Anderson, George Keyworth, nuclear physicist Edward Teller, and
Edwin Thomas, Meese's assistant. "Not only did everyone feel we

should pursue the idea of missile defense," Anderson recalled, "they also deeply believed it could be done." There was general agreement that a major part of a missile defense effort would "probably" be based in space, and that an effective missile defense effort "could defend not only our population and cities, but also our offensive nuclear missiles." A smaller follow-up meeting took place on October 12, and included Meese, Ed Thomas, Anderson, General Graham and Bendetsen. The latter two reported growing support and interest in the idea from members of Congress, the National Aeronautics and Space Administration, the CIA, the Air Force and the Department of Defense. Their status report was encouraging and even "glowing."[136]

Meese decided it was time to go directly to the President, and on January 8, 1982, the informal missile defense group met with Reagan in the Roosevelt Room; the meeting was not listed on the President's official schedule. The outside advisers included Teller, Bendetsen, and kitchen cabinet members Jacquelin (Jack) Hume, William Wilson, and Joseph Coors. Representing the White House were Meese, Anderson, Keyworth and William Clark, who had been serving as deputy secretary of state and had just been named the new national security adviser. Originally scheduled for fifteen minutes, the "animated" meeting lasted for almost an hour. Meese remembers the tenor of the discussion as "highly favorable," so much so that Reagan directed the National Security Council staff to develop a proposal for a strategic defense initiative.[137]

A critical turning point in the creation of SDI was a meeting between the President and the Joint Chiefs of Staff in December 1982, at which Reagan asked his top military advisers, "What if ... we began to move away from our total reliance on offense to deter a

The White House

Meese with Mrs. Anwar Sadat and First Lady Nancy Reagan, circa 1983.

nuclear attack and moved toward a relatively greater reliance on defense?" As the President continued to press the issue, "small lights
and bells" began to go off in the minds of the Joint Chiefs, and one
of them later telephoned Bill Clark. "Did we just get instructions to
take a hard look at missile defense?" "Yes," replied Clark, and the
Joint Chiefs had their marching orders.[138]

On March 23, 1983, President Reagan announced in a nationally
televised address (drafted by Deputy National Security Adviser
Robert McFarlane) that development and deployment of a comprehensive antiballistic missile system would be his top defense pri-

ority—his "ultimate goal." "I call upon the scientific community in our country," he said, "those who gave us nuclear weapons, to turn their great talents now to the cause of mankind and world peace, to give us the means of rendering these nuclear weapons impotent and obsolete." SDI was immediately ridiculed as "Star Wars" by liberal detractors, led by Democratic Senator Edward Kennedy. *The New York Times* called the initiative "a pipe dream, a projection of fantasy into policy."[139]

But the vehement protest of Soviet leader Yuri Andropov suggested that Soviet scientists regarded SDI not as a fantasy but a technological feat they could not match. General Vladimir Slipchenko, a leading military scientist who served on the Soviet General Staff, recalled that SDI put the military "in a state of fear and shock." General Makhmut Gareev, who headed the department of strategic analysis in the Soviet Ministry of Defense, later revealed what he had told the Soviet general staff and the Politburo in 1983: "Not only could we not defeat SDI, SDI defeated all our possible countermeasures."[140] More than any other strategic action he took, Reagan's tenacious commitment to SDI forced the Soviet Union to come to the bargaining table and enabled America to win the Cold War without firing a shot. And the process began with a meeting in Ed Meese's office.

Like Reagan, Meese knew the value of humor in defusing the inevitable tension of the policymaking process. At one session the troika of Baker, Meese, and Deaver held with cabinet members, all participants, following a long debate, agreed on a paper that summarized positions Reagan would take with Third World leaders at a conference. But Secretary of State Alexander Haig then asserted, "I've got one last change to make." According to *Time*, Meese replied, deadpan, "No, Al, we're not going to take out the words, 'The President.'" Even Haig joined in the laughter.[141]

Although there was limited interest among other senior aides about social issues such as abortion and school prayer, Meese helped keep the social agenda alive by arranging for leaders of the Religious Right to meet frequently with the President and by lending his name to the cause, as when he agreed to serve as honorary chairman of the Congress on the Bible in March 1982. Bill Bright of Campus Crusade for Christ International praised Meese for "the tremendous role" he was playing as Counsellor to the President and thanked him for agreeing to be the keynote speaker at the Congress. Addressing the estimated 5,000 delegates, Meese sounded more than a little like the President when he remarked, "Someone has estimated that throughout the course of history man has adopted over four billion laws. It seems to me, with all that effort, we haven't improved one iota on the Ten Commandments."[142]

Meese was with President Reagan when he gave his historic June 1982 address to the British Parliament in Westminster and predicted that Communism was headed for "the ash heap of history." And he was with Reagan on his November 1983 visit to South Korea and the Demilitarized Zone (DMZ) when the President thanked troops of the 2nd Infantry Division for serving on "the frontlines of freedom." He recalled the events of August 1976, when ax-wielding North Korean troops had crossed the DMZ and killed two U.S. Army officers. "Let me state for the record— and I know you feel the same way," Reagan said sternly, "nothing like that better happen again."[143]

Meese's years as Counsellor to the President were not an unbroken succession of triumphs. There were political setbacks like

Ed and Ursula Meese with Ed's parents, Edwin Meese, Jr., and Leone Meese, 1985.

TEFRA (the Tax Equity and Fiscal Responsibility Act of 1982), which President Reagan approved with the understanding that Congress would approve three dollars in spending cuts for every dollar of tax increase. The $98 billion in new taxes were immediately implemented, but the Democratic Congress wound up cutting less than twenty-seven cents for every new tax dollar. Meese called TEFRA "the greatest domestic error of the Reagan administration," although it did leave untouched—at the White House's insistence—the individual tax rate reductions of the Economic Recovery and Tax Act of the previous year.[144] As a result of TEFRA, the President learned to "trust but verify"—not only when dealing with the Soviets but also with Congress.

There was the "summer of the long knives" in 1982 when *Time*,

Newsweek, The Washington Post, and other mainstream media decided that Ed Meese had been toppled from power and was a member of the White House troika in name only. *The Washingtonian* magazine said, "Nobody knows what he does except stay on the good side of the President."[145] But Meese declined to play the Washington game. He did not leak denigrating stories about other senior aides. He did not take Washington columnists to lunch and gossip about the President. He *did* sit down with a few reporters and, in his direct but affable way, discuss the official agenda of the Reagan Administration. As for the stories that he was no longer "deputy president," Meese told one reporter briskly that the press had exaggerated his role when he first arrived in Washington and that the recent stories about his "diminished" role were "equally untrue."[146] "His job is just what it's been all along," said White House communications chief David Gergen. "He's a tremendously influential and highly valued adviser to the President who advises on issues across the board.... He's one of the men who has known [the President] so long and so well he's become almost an alter ego of Ronald Reagan."[147]

The top 3,000 presidential appointees of the Reagan Administration publicly demonstrated that they shared Gergen's opinion. At the annual Executive Forum, held in Constitution Hall and intended to build morale throughout the Administration, each member of the cabinet would enter one by one to be greeted by applause. "The one person who always brought the house down," Kenneth Cribb remembers, "was Ed Meese. It was as much of a poll of the administration as you could get. And it happened every time."[148]

The personal parallels between the President and his Counsellor had long been evident. Each had a laid-back temperament but a formidable work ethic. Each was eternally optimistic and always saw the best in everyone. Each had a strong faith that showed itself in deeds as well as words. Each stuck to his principles and was not easily moved once he had made up his mind. They were modest about their accomplishments and comfortable with being underestimated. They had a subtle, almost telepathic relationship, developed by years of interaction. Pen James recalls a meeting in the Oval Office where, as usual, Meese sat opposite Reagan so that he had direct eye contact with him. "Once," James remembers, "when they were discussing a key point, Ed lifted his head, and the President caught his eye, and Ed nodded ever so slightly. It was clear to me that Reagan was wondering what Ed thought. I marveled at the chemistry," James says.[149]

They differed in that Ronald Reagan had been a movement conservative since the mid-1950s, spreading the conservative gospel from 1954 to 1962 as General Electric's spokesman, reading *Human Events* and *National Review*, lending his name to organizations like Young Americans for Freedom and Fred Schwarz's Christian Anti-Communism Crusade, and campaigning enthusiastically in 1964 for presidential candidate Barry Goldwater.

In his early professional years, Ed Meese had been steadfastly apolitical. Influenced by his father's exemplary career, Ed Meese regarded himself as a public servant dedicated to the public good, whether as a deputy district attorney or as chief of staff to a governor. While his philosophy was generally conservative, reflecting his Lutheran faith, it was not Conservative. His guiding document was the U.S. Constitution, not *The Conservative Mind*. But working every day with Ronald Reagan can change a man. The transition from objective public servant to loyal Reagan aide to eloquent leader of the conservative movement took some fifteen years, but by 1982,

Ed Meese was expounding the intrinsic worth of the individual and the free market—while wearing an Adam Smith tie—at dozens of conservative meetings, large and small, across the country.

One of Meese's most enduring contributions to the conservative movement—and the American legal landscape—was his early and generous support of the Federalist Society. Today the Society has more than 200 chapters (60 for lawyers, 145 at law schools); serves as a recruiting source for the freedom-based public interest law movement; publishes the *Harvard Journal of Law and Public Policy*; and sponsors meetings and symposia featuring federal and state judges, journalists, law professors, and prominent lawyers. In the early 1980s, the Society was just an idea of three young law students who had known each other in college: Steven Calabresi at Yale and David McIntosh and Lee Lieberman at the University of Chicago. They joined forces with Spencer Abraham, a student at Harvard Law School. They received encouragement from two professors— Ralph Winter of Yale, now a senior judge on the Court of Appeals for the Second Circuit, and Antonin Scalia of Chicago, now a Supreme Court Justice.

"Ed Meese understood that ideas have consequences in law as well as in other areas of public policy," says Calabresi, who served as a special assistant to Attorney General Meese from 1985-1987 and is today a professor of law at Northwestern University. "He saw that the Federalist Society could spread the message of the Reagan administration to the campuses," Calabresi says. "Through his speeches and his appearances before Society chapters he energized our members to push for conservative reform." Meese even helped the Federalist Society secure the ultimate speaker for its September 1988 national conference—President Reagan. "Ed Meese was pivotal in bringing the Federalist Society forward," says its executive vice president Leonard Leo, and served as "a mentor to our founders." As Attorney General, he "gave ideas like original meaning legitimacy and helped build credibility for the conservative legal movement." And he has continued to be involved with the Society, whether as a member of the Board of Visitors or as a featured speaker. "He truly has done whatever he could," says president Eugene B. Meyer.[150]

A TIME OF TESTING

Ed Meese's deeply rooted faith was tested in the extreme when his 19-year-old son Scott, home from college, was killed in late July 1982 in a single-car accident in northern Virginia. Meese was in San Francisco on official business when Lyn Nofziger awakened him in the middle of the night to give him, reluctantly, the terrible news. "He bent over and groaned deeply," Nofziger recalls, "and then he straightened up and began making calls. He took charge. He had to because Ursula was out of the country." Meese took the first plane available back to Washington, D.C. He was in his White House office less than five minutes when the President and Mrs. Reagan walked in and put their arms around him. "They literally wept with me," Meese wrote later, "and consoled me at the worst time in my life." "It was the only time," says Kenneth Cribb, "I ever saw Mrs. Reagan in the West Wing." Both of the Reagans attended the funeral and then invited the Meese family to use Camp David for several days "to get our lives back together."[151]

At Scott's funeral and at the reception afterwards in their home,

Meese Family Collection

The Meese family, 1981: Scott, Dana, Ursula, Ed, and Michael.

Ed and Ursula Meese spent much of their time consoling family and friends, especially their son, Michael, a recent West Point graduate, and their daughter, Dana, who was living at home while attending a girls' school. "Their religious faith took them through it," says John Herrington. "They strengthened one another," says

Pen James, remarking, "What should a marriage look like? Look at Ed and Ursula."[152] At about this time, Meese joined a Bible study fellowship group started by the late Herb Ellingwood, one of his closest friends, which included Doug Coe, coordinator of the National Prayer Breakfast, and General John Vessey, chairman of the Joint Chiefs of Staff. With very few exceptions, Meese has attended every Tuesday morning gathering for the last two decades.

After a week off with his family, Ed Meese was back in the White House and working on the President's agenda. At the top was the selection of federal judges. The Administration was resolved that judges should be arbiters rather than policymakers. Many of the controversial issues confronting the nation—such as abortion, prayer in schools, pornography, busing, and leniency toward crime—had resulted from federal court decisions during the previous twenty years. For the President and his advisers, the answer was to restore the proper role of the judiciary. Relying upon the model he had instituted in California, Reagan determined to choose federal judges who respected the written Constitution and were highly qualified, not simply cronies of political supporters.

At the center of the process was the Committee on Federal Judicial Selection, formed in 1981. Chaired by White House counsel Fred Fielding, the committee included Ed Meese, Jim Baker, Attorney General William French Smith, Pen James, Assistant Attorney General for Legal Policy Jonathan Rose, and Kenneth Cribb (when he became Meese's principal assistant). Complementing the White House committee was the Office of Legal Policy that Smith established in the Justice Department. Also deeply involved in researching candidates was Kenneth W. Starr, counselor to the Attorney General. The two groups looked for nominees who not only received good ratings from the American Bar Association and could rattle off phrases like "judicial restraint" and "strict construction" but could pass a rigorous examination about the philosophy underlying strict construction. The judicial candidates were not subjected to "political litmus questions" about abortion, the death penalty or anything else, but the questioning was as serious, according to one participant, "as for any Rhodes scholar."[153] Critics alleged that the search for judges committed to a philosophy of "judicial restraint" was an attempt to "politicize" the courts. But in fact Reagan was seeking the opposite end—to de-politicize the courts so that they played a truly judicial role rather than, as Ed Meese put it, "usurping the authority of the elected branches of our constitutional system."[154]

The President succeeded, perhaps even beyond his expectations—thanks in large measure to Ed Meese, who played a principal role in judicial selection throughout the Reagan presidency, first as Counsellor to the President and then as Attorney General. Over the course of his two Administrations, Reagan appointed almost half of the federal judiciary—368 judges out of a total of 761—more than any other president in history and a higher percentage of the judiciary than any president except Franklin D. Roosevelt. Reagan also named a Chief Justice of the Supreme Court and three associate justices.

The qualifications of Reagan's federal judges, said political scientist and legal expert Sheldon Goldman of the University of Massachusetts, were above those of the judges appointed by his four predecessors—Carter, Ford, Nixon, and Johnson. Writing shortly after Reagan left office, Goldman concluded that President Reagan would have the greatest influence on the American judiciary and law of any president since FDR, leaving "a judicial legacy [that] will be with us well into the next century." Appraising that legacy fifteen years later, analyst Tony Mauro wrote in the *Legal Times* that Reagan "forever changed the judicial nominating process."[155]

Given Meese's unique relationship with Reagan over the years and his extensive legal background as prosecutor, lawyer, and law professor, it was not surprising that when Attorney General Bill Smith told the President in early 1984 that he wanted to return to California, Reagan immediately nominated Edwin Meese III to succeed him as the 75th Attorney General of the United States. "Ed is not only my trusted Counsellor," the President said, but a person "whose life and experience reflect a profound commitment to the law and a consistent dedication to the improvement of our justice system."[156] What was surprising was the vehemence of the opposition to Ed Meese.

Senate Democrats tied up the nomination for thirteen months, raising so many questions about the prospective attorney general's finances and other actions (such as a gift of cufflinks from South Korea that Meese put in his basement and promptly forgot about), that Meese himself requested an independent counsel (the successor to the "special prosecutor" of the Watergate era) to investigate the allegations. While it was clear that Senate liberals such as Howard Metzenbaum of Ohio strongly opposed Ed Meese's law-and-order philosophy, his criticism of the ACLU and other sacred cows, and his general conservatism, their true target was President Reagan, engaged in a highly successful reelection campaign. Unable to defeat him at the polls, they hoped to damage Reagan by roughing up his most faithful aide and Counsellor whom they accused of "political

Meese Family Collection

Chief Justice Warren Burger swears in Edwin Meese III as Attorney General
of the United States, February 1985.

back-scratching and cronyism." The President was scornful of the
tactic, privately writing a friend, "There is no doubt this is a lynching
of the innocent." Asked at a March 13, 1984, news conference whether the American people would be able to trust Meese as Attorney
General, Reagan replied, "I trust him more than some of the Senators that have been raising these issues." The President reinforced
his commitment later that month when a reporter inquired, "Has
[Meese] offered to step aside?" "No," Reagan said, "and I wouldn't
listen if he did."[157] The nominee himself pledged that he would not
seek to have his name withdrawn, explaining, "I intend to pursue the
vindication of my name, the honor of my family, and the confidence
of the President of the United States in nominating me."[158]

In September 1984, Independent Counsel Jacob Stein reported that after an exhaustive six-month investigation involving interviews with over 200 witnesses (including Ed and Ursula Meese) and the examination of thousands of documents, he had found "no basis" for prosecution against Ed Meese for any of the allegations against him. Among the specific findings was that although a friend who made loans to Ursula Meese received a government job, he had obtained the job "without the knowledge of (or any intervention by) Mr. Meese." A savings and loan decision to extend his mortgages rather than foreclosing was "sound from a business point of view." Regarding his promotion in the Army, a confidential Army Inspector General Report stated that "not only did Mr. Meese not ask for special consideration in his behalf, he specifically requested that he not be accorded such consideration."[159] Four months after the release of Stein's findings, the director of the Office of Government Ethics ruled that Meese had committed no ethical violations.

Ed Meese "is one of the most decent and honorable men I've ever known," said President Reagan, "so I'm not surprised by the outcome." He promised that if reelected, he would resubmit Meese's nomination as Attorney General in January 1985. Despite Reagan's landslide victory, the Democrats continued their vendetta against Ed Meese. At a confirmation hearing of the Senate Judiciary Committee in February, Democrat Joseph Biden of Delaware told Meese—in a speech described by one newspaper as "one of the smarmiest, most reprehensible and self-indulgent" delivered in a Senate hearing room in 30 years—that while Meese had done no criminal wrong and he didn't believe him to be unethical, he considered his behavior to be "beneath the office" of Attorney General. Aiming as low as he could, Democrat Patrick Leahy of Vermont

Senator sarcastically asked the nominee, "Was there anyone who made loans to you since you came to Washington who didn't receive a job in Washington?"[160] *The Wall Street Journal* correctly charged that the Senate Judiciary Committee's Democrats were not conducting a confirmation hearing but "attempting to destroy" someone with whom they disagreed. They were allowing "half-truths and innuendo all to appear day after day as an unproven indictment." Someone, editorialized the *Journal*, needed to ask, "Sir, have you no decency?"[161]

Throughout the long crucible of nomination and confirmation, the one man who demonstrated beyond any question his decency and his fortitude was Ed Meese. He never once complained, publicly or privately, about the unfair and even cruel treatment he received in the Senate and in the media. When those around him wanted to respond in kind, he refused. Such an exchange, he explained, would only detract from what the President was seeking to accomplish. He later joked about the ordeal, saying, "Not such a bad record—nominated in February, confirmed in March."[162] He never contemplated giving up because he knew he was innocent of any wrongdoing—because his withdrawal would be used by the President's critics, and because he had an agenda he was eager to implement as Attorney General. Not even his most implacable opponents guessed how ambitious that agenda was.

At last, on February 23, 1985, in a rare Saturday session, the U.S. Senate voted 63-31 to confirm Edwin Meese III as Attorney General. "I think that politics played a very big part in what took place," Meese said in his understated way, while pointing out that he had been approved by a two-to-one margin. "But that's all behind us," he said. "I am committed to the fair, compassionate and forward-looking policies the department should have."[163] Without pause, Ed Meese set about showing what he meant by fair and compassionate, beginning with an emphasis on the rights of victims and the importance of according a proper respect for the original meaning of the Constitution.

Chapter V

BRINGING JUSTICE
TO THE PEOPLE

~~

While not the largest federal agency in Washington, the Department of Justice in 1985 had 72,000 employees, an annual budget of $3.6 billion, and far-ranging responsibilities from law enforcement and civil rights to immigration and judicial selection. It included some of the best known and influential federal agencies, such as the Federal Bureau of Investigation, the U.S. Marshals Service, the Federal Bureau of Prisons, the Immigration and Naturalization Service, and the Drug Enforcement Administration. According to the official mission statement of the department, the Attorney General was expected to enforce the law and defend the interests of the United States, ensure public safety against threats foreign and domestic, provide leadership in preventing and controlling crime, seek just punishment for the guilty, administer and enforce the immigration laws, and "ensure fair and impartial administration of justice for all Americans." Even for Ed Meese, who liked to keep busy, it was a Herculean list. What made it even more challenging was that Meese remained in close and often daily contact with the

President as chairman of the Cabinet Council on Domestic Policy and an attendee of National Security Council meetings.

While the protection of citizens from violent crime is essentially a function of state and local government, the federal government has a distinct role in it. For example, the Department of Justice under Meese and his predecessor, William French Smith, repeatedly tried to combat unreasonable restrictions on the use of pertinent evidence in criminal trials. Because of the so-called exclusionary rule, Meese said, the courts were throwing out "perfectly valid evidence"—such as illegal drugs or stolen property discovered in the possession of a suspect—if the police had made some minor procedural error. Thus, as Justice Benjamin Cardozo once put it, "the criminal is to go free because the constable has blundered." The proper way to ensure good procedure by the police, Meese argued, was to discipline those law enforcement people who violated the law—"not bar the use of evidence that would help determine the truth."[164] Also, the Meese Justice Department argued for tougher and more effective sentencing of recidivist criminals responsible for much of the nation's crime and pushed for the construction of additional prison space so that convicted criminals could be isolated from society.

Some observers say that the Reagan Administration brought about a fundamental change in the criminal justice system through its emphasis on the rights of victims—a longtime concern of Ed Meese. As Counsellor to the President, he pushed hard to establish the President's Task Force on Victims of Crime, headed by Assistant Attorney General Lois Haight (Herrington), who, like Meese, had been a deputy district attorney in Alameda County. Following the task force's recommendations, Congress passed the Federal

The White House

Ed and Ursula Meese join President Reagan
for a Thanksgiving holiday, circa 1981.

Victim/Witness Protection Act of 1982 and the Victims of Crime
Assistance Act of 1984. "Victims now have the right to be present
and speak when judges pass sentence," says Haight, who has been a
California state judge since 1993. That was not the case before Reagan was elected president. "Ed was extremely supportive of our task
force," she adds. "I briefed the cabinet twice on victims of crime."[165]

During the 1980s, no issue of law enforcement prompted greater
concern than drug abuse, the accompanying toll in crime and death,
and the ruined lives of the addicted. Both in the White House and
the Justice Department, said Meese, "we conducted an all-out offensive to combat narcotics trafficking and abuse." One important
and highly visible part of the effort was Nancy Reagan's "Just Say

No To Drugs" campaign. The President adopted a "zero toler-ance" policy toward all drugs, enabling Justice to emphasize that marijuana was not only illegal and harmful in itself but also a "gate-way" drug that often led to other forms of drug abuse. The estab-lishment of drug-free schools and workplaces was encouraged and, at the same time, the number of drug treatment and rehabilitation facilities was expanded.

Cooperative actions with the governments of drug-producing countries such as Bolivia and Colombia were undertaken while in-terdiction along the U.S. borders was dramatically stepped up. "One of our most effective weapons against drug traffickers," Meese said, "was to confiscate the assets of their criminal activity" such as auto-mobiles, yachts, homes, and businesses.[166] Helping to coordinate all these activities was the cabinet-level National Drug Policy Board, which Meese chaired.

As a result of the Reagan Administration's firm stand against drugs, the annual use of any illicit drug by high school seniors dropped from 54 percent in 1979 to 29 percent in 1991, a decrease of over 45 percent. Annual use among college students from 1980 to 1991 fell over 48 percent. The 1991 statistics showed that 90 per-cent of high school seniors disapproved of even trying LSD, barbi-turates, cocaine, or heroin, while nearly 70 percent disapproved of trying marijuana—a sharp break from the experimental attitudes shaped by the permissive drug culture of the 1960s.

The Reagan Administration also initiated a major effort to com-bat both international and domestic terrorism. Civil libertarians in-sisted that law enforcement officials could move against the actions of terrorists only after they had happened. One group that benefit-ed from this utopian view was the Weather Underground, which in the 1960s had been involved in riots, bombings, bank robberies, and other acts of terrorism. To prevent further violence, FBI agents intercepted telephone messages of a known Weather Underground contact by entering the premises of the group. Two agents of the FBI were accused of violating the civil liberties of the terrorists, indicted, and convicted by the Carter Justice Department.

To Ed Meese and President Reagan, this was "an unconscionable perversion of the justice process," and at Meese's suggestion, Reagan granted a presidential pardon to agents Mark Felt and Edward Miller. Reagan's forthright action sent an unequivocal message that America had a chief executive and an administration that would "stand with the people who took on the difficult and often dangerous task of defending society from violent criminals and revolutionaries," while at the same time "protecting our basic liberties."[167] It was a message that Ed Meese reinforced throughout his tenure as Attorney General through direct contact with police executives, sheriffs, and district attorneys around the nation. As with street crime and drugs, the Reagan Administration effectively deterred terrorism: The number of terrorist incidents in the U.S. dropped from 112 in 1977 to just seven in 1985 and eight in 1986. In 1985 alone, the FBI detected and prevented twenty-three terrorist missions within America's borders without violating anyone's civil liberties.

Near the end of his first term, President Reagan met with a group of religious leaders and child welfare experts who explained that "a flood of obscene material was sweeping across the nation" and affecting in particular the nation's young people.[168] Deeply disturbed by what he heard, the President asked Attorney General Smith to appoint a Commission on Pornography to examine the problem and recommend how law enforcement agencies and others should deal with it. Shortly after he became Attorney General, Meese formally appointed the Commission and charged its members to provide the President, the executive branch, and Congress with a comprehensive evaluation.

A year later, the Commission delivered its disturbing report: (1) Obscene materials and child pornography were pervasive throughout America's communities. (2) Pornography was causing extensive social harm, especially among the young. (3) There were close ties between the obscenity industry and organized crime. (4) Very little law enforcement action was being taken against the sale and distribution of obscene materials because they were not regarded as serious offenses when compared with street crime and drugs. The Meese Justice Department immediately began implementing the Commission's recommendations, starting with the creation of the Obscenity Enforcement Unit in the Criminal Division. Legislation was written to present to Congress. Model statutes were developed for the states. As a result, there was a sharp increase in investigations and prosecutions of obscenity and child pornography offenses at the federal and state levels, along with greater public awareness of the grave social harm caused by pornography.

In the field of civil rights, the President was adamant that the administration crack down on hate crime, discrimination, and organized bigotry. The Meese Justice Department, with the President's concurrence, insisted that justice should be administered impartially without reference to skin color, gender, religion, or ethnic origin. Ironically, this color-blind civil rights policy, endorsed by Martin Luther King, Jr., and other civil rights leaders of the 1950s and 1960s, was opposed by civil rights advocates of the 1970s and 1980s. They insisted that skin color and other attributes should be the basis for special treatment of certain citizens. "This was the essence," Meese wrote, "of various 'affirmative action,' quota, minority-set-aside, and other schemes." The impact of such practices as school busing on authentic civil rights was devastating. In a society that was allegedly color-blind and impartial in dealing with all its citizens, Meese pointed out, people were singled out for different treatment "precisely because of their color or ethnic origin," while others were turned away because of theirs.[169]

The Reagan Administration emphatically disagreed with this violation of two basic principles of a free society. All people should be treated equally under the law, and advancement should be based on merit, rather than racial, ethnic, or other distinctions. The position provoked bitter controversy between the Administration and the civil rights establishment, but neither Reagan nor Meese backed down.

The Great Debate

At the core of President Reagan's concept of limited government and American freedom was the original Constitution which, in the view of the President and advisers like Ed Meese, provided the indispensable political framework for a free society. In Reagan's view, as political scientist Andrew E. Busch put it, the Constitution was a living document but could only remain so "if its meaning was predictable from day to day." The President quoted Madison: "[If] the sense in which the Constitution was accepted and ratified by the nation is not the guide to expounding it, there can be no security for a faithful exercise of its powers."[170] Accordingly, Attorney General

Meese set about crafting an ambitious agenda for legal reform and judicial selection based upon the Constitution of 1787.

In a speech to the American Bar Association in July 1985, just five months after taking office as Attorney General, Meese asserted that the Supreme Court had engaged in too much policymaking in its latest term and showed too little "deference to what the Constitution—its text and intonation—may demand." It was fair to conclude, he said, that far too many of the Court's opinions were "more policy choices than articulations of long-term constitutional principles." The high court, Meese said, should employ a "Jurisprudence of Original Intention"—a return to the intent of the authors of the Constitution and the Bill of Rights.[171] One analyst said that Meese was the first Attorney General since Robert Jackson under Franklin Roosevelt to enter into the debate as to how the Constitution ought to be interpreted and to recognize that "there is a central role for the executive branch in shaping the form of jurisprudence."[172]

A week later, the Department of Justice filed a "friend of the court" brief with the Supreme Court asking that the 1973 *Roe v. Wade* decision legalizing abortion on demand be overturned. And in a speech to the Knights of Columbus, the largest Catholic lay group in America, Meese argued that it "begs credulity" that American values cannot be "religious in nature." By removing from public education and discourse all references to traditional religion and substituting the morality of the cult of self, he warned, "we run the risk of subordinating all other religions to a new secular religion which is a far cry from the traditional values . . . which underlie the American people."[173]

The reactions of the proponents of a "living constitution" ranged from incredulous to furious. They protested that the Meese Justice

Department was engaging in a "badly disguised attempt" to limit the constitutional rights of minorities. They hailed Associate Justice William J. Brennan, Jr., when he publicly described the constitutional views endorsed by Ed Meese as "little more than arrogance cloaked as humility." Vigorously defending the judicial activism he practiced, Brennan stressed the need to adapt the Constitution "to cope with current problems and current needs."[174] The Attorney General calmly responded that he welcomed Justice Brennan to the widening debate over the Constitution and its application. "There is a sense that a sea change is upon us," commented A.E. Dick Howard, a professor of law at the University of Virginia, and "Mr. Meese is willing to lead the charge."[175]

Another prominent participant in the debate was Robert Bork, a member of the D.C. Court of Appeals, and a former professor of law at Yale. "All theories that do not rest on the concept of original intent," Bork argued, "are political theories." A judge who "applies the morality of our time," he said, "will end up applying his or her own morality. Original intent takes the values of the framers and applies them to today's changing problems. It's not easy, it's not mechanical, but it's also not impossible."[176]

The Attorney General reiterated the theme of "original intention" with a November speech to the D.C. chapter of the Federalist Society, saying that interpreting the Constitution's "spirit" instead of its words invited the danger of "seeing the Constitution as an empty vessel into which each generation may pour its passion and prejudice." He charged that the current judicial activism was not faithful to the written Constitution. "An activist jurisprudence, one which anchors the Constitution only in the consciences of jurists," he added, "is a chameleon jurisprudence, changing color and form in each era." A true approach, Meese said, "must respect the Constitution in all its parts and be faithful to the Constitution in its entirety." He recalled the words of the late Justice Felix Frankfurter:

> [T]here is not under our Constitution a judicial remedy for every political mischief, for every undesirable exercise of legislative power. The framers carefully and with deliberate forethought refused to enthrone the judiciary. In this situation, as in others of like nature, appeal for relief does not belong here. Appeal must be made to an informed, civically militant electorate.[177]

Ed Meese shocked the Left again with his October 1986 talk at Tulane University when he stated that a Supreme Court decision "does not establish 'a supreme law of the land' that is binding on all persons and parts of the government, henceforth and forevermore." He was on firm ground: After all, Lincoln led a war to overturn the Court's decision in *Dred Scott*, which said Congress could not stop slavery in the territories. The Attorney General said that there is a difference between constitutional law—the rulings of the Court—and the Constitution. If you don't like something in the Constitution, your only recourse is an amendment. But if you don't like a Court ruling, as *The Wall Street Journal* pointed out, "you can try to get the justices to reverse themselves."[178] And the high court had overruled 230 of its decisions in the first two hundred years of its existence.

The officials of each branch take oaths to enforce the Constitution. The goal, said Meese, was "to maintain the important function of judicial review while at the same time upholding the right of people to govern themselves through the democratic branches of government." That is, Congress, the President, and the states are free to encourage the Supreme Court to reconsider its opinions. Ed Meese was immediately castigated by liberals such as Ira Glasser of the American Civil Liberties Union, who said that the Meese address was an "invitation to lawlessness." The head of the American Bar Association harrumphed that acknowledging the power of other branches to interpret the Constitution "shakes the foundation of the system." Apparently he had forgotten what Jefferson wrote: The Constitution no more gives judges the "right to decide for the executive . . . than to the executive to decide for them."

Liberals like Glasser conveniently overlooked what one of their own kind, Harvard law professor Laurence Tribe, wrote in his constitutional law textbook: "Despite the growth of federal judicial power, the Constitution remains a fundamentally democratic document, open to competing interpretations limited only by the values which inform the Constitution's provisions themselves, and by the complex political process that the Constitution creates—a process which on various occasions gives the Supreme Court, Congress, the President, or the states, the last word in constitutional debate."[179] All Attorney General Meese was suggesting was that judges respect the text of the Constitution and the intent of the Founders who wrote it.

With the backing of the President, Meese also stressed the importance of restoring the checks and balances of the structural Constitution, especially the principles of federalism and separation of powers. The Federalism Task Force, suggested by Meese, developed several proposals to re-limit the national government to its enumerated powers. The effort culminated in Executive Order

The White House

Meese at the White House with President Reagan and Secretary of Defense
Caspar Weinberger, circa 1986.

12612 in October 1987, which required executive agencies to undertake "federalism assessments" before taking major actions and to
consider ways to avoid preempting state law whenever possible.

The President also supported the Justice Department's remarkable series of seminars on the Constitution. Academics, Justice officials, and prominent lawyers discussed not a specific bill or regulation but how the Constitution applied to the entire business of
government and how to ensure that the Constitution would become
part of the decision-making process throughout the government.

"The Meese Justice Department," says Kenneth Cribb, "became the brain trust of the whole administration."[180] One result of the brain-trusting was a series of reports—so-called blue books because they were bound in blue—released by the Office of Legal Policy, headed by Stephen J. Markman from 1985 to 1989, on constitutional issues such as search and seizure and religious liberty. The latter, for example, concluded that the original meaning of the Free Exercise Clause (as incorporated by the Fourteenth Amendment) is to deprive "state and federal governments from forbidding or preventing . . . the free exercise of sincerely-held religious beliefs."[181]

Another Meese initiative was the research and writing of major studies by the Domestic Policy Council on several of the most challenging issues of modern America, such as welfare reform, the environment, the family, federalism, and privatization. Becky Norton Dunlop, who served as director of the Cabinet office and then senior special assistant for council affairs, says that Ed Meese selected or appointed the people to head the task forces or working groups that produced the papers. She explains, "He wanted to set down where we had been, where we were, and where we should be going."[182] The welfare study outlined a new national public assistance strategy that emphasized community-based and state-sponsored projects. The family report stated that "family policy must be built upon a foundation of economic growth," meaning "low marginal tax rates, keeping inflation under control, and resisting federal spending that undermines 'household prosperity.'" The federalism report stated that constitutional federalism in America had been "eviscerated" and that the national government should adopt a "non-intervention policy regarding matters properly within the constitutional powers reserved to the States."[183]

Never before had any Attorney General given so much careful attention to the building of an intellectual foundation for the policymakers of an administration. In so acting, Ed Meese demonstrated that he spanned the world of ideas and the world of politics much as the Founders of the Republic had. "One of my heroes," says law professor Steven Calabresi, "is James Madison, and Ed Meese is like Madison in his abiding interest not simply in ideas but in the implementation of ideas."[184]

Picking the Right Judges

The administration's goal in judicial selection, Ed Meese said candidly, was "to institutionalize the Reagan Revolution so it can't be set aside no matter what happens in future presidential elections." Helping him at Justice was a brilliant, youthful brain trust that included T. Kenneth Cribb, Jr., Counsellor to the Attorney General; Terry Eastland, Meese's official spokesman; Grover Rees III, who coordinated the screening of judicial candidates; Garry McDowell, who supervised the speechwriting team; William Bradford Reynolds, Assistant Attorney General for Civil Rights; Stephen J. Markman, assistant attorney general for the Office of Legal Policy; and John Richardson, Meese's chief of staff.

Attorneys general have been advising presidents on judicial selection since the 1850s, but the Meese Justice Department, in the words of legal scholar Sheldon Goldman, engaged in the "most systematic judicial philosophical screening of judicial candidates ever seen in the nation's history."[185] For the first time, all leading candidates were brought to Washington, D.C., for extensive questioning by members of the Meese team. Simply put, the department sought judges who believed in judicial restraint and the rule of law rather than the rule of judges. Irrelevant were the candidate's political activity or ideology, his views about controversial issues such as abortion or school prayer. Very relevant, Terry Eastland explained, were his views about federalism and the separation of powers, and his "approaches to constitutional and legal interpretation."[186] The Meese Justice Department also used actuarial tables in its evaluations, determined to place on the bench "younger, vigorous, more aggressive supporters of the administration's judicial philosophy." The goal, wrote Goldman, was to create a lasting Reagan legacy on the lower courts "second only to the U.S. Supreme Court."[187] At Meese's suggestion, President Reagan personally telephoned every judicial nominee, reinforcing the importance of the appointment.

President Reagan dramatically shifted the philosophical makeup of the high court by appointing Associate Justices Sandra Day O'Connor, Antonin Scalia, and Anthony Kennedy and elevating William Rehnquist to Chief Justice. O'Connor, an Arizona appeals court judge and former state senator, was the first woman named to the Supreme Court. In appointing her, Reagan fulfilled a campaign promise. Reagan's next Supreme Court opportunity came five years later. In late May or early June 1986, Kenneth Cribb recalls, Chief Justice Warren Burger informed Ed Meese that he would be resigning. Meese turned to Brad Reynolds, whom he had already instructed to draw up a list of possible appointees in case a vacancy occurred on the Court. Reynolds had assigned Justice officials to research in depth the background of twenty prospective justices.

Scalia, a U.S. Court of Appeals judge, and Robert Bork, a member of the same court, were "hands down" the best candidates, says

Cribb. Meese presented both of their names to the President, who picked Scalia because he was eight years younger than Bork. He was also an Italian-American and would be the first ever of Italian ancestry to sit on the Court. Meese recommended that Rehnquist, arguably the court's most conservative member, be elevated to chief justice, and Reagan agreed. The President told Meese that he would give Bork the next vacancy. Back in his office at the Justice Department, Meese was openly "ecstatic" over the President's decisions, and Cribb broke out the sherry for his boss and Brad Reynolds, toasting the President and the Supreme Court.[188] With Republicans in the majority, the Senate confirmed Scalia unanimously, but thirty-three Senate liberals led by Edward Kennedy voted against Rehnquist—the most votes cast against any justice or chief justice confirmed in the twentieth century. The anti-Rehnquist vote was the tip of a liberal iceberg that would sink the President's next nomination to the court.

When Justice Lewis Powell resigned in June 1987, Ed Meese quietly reminded President Reagan of his pledge to fill the next Court vacancy with Robert Bork, which the President promptly did. But the political calculus had drastically changed. The Democrats had recaptured the Senate in November 1986 and now controlled the nomination process. The White House was preoccupied with trying to contain the political fallout of the Iran-Contra affair. And the Administration was unprepared for the well-organized and well-financed campaign conducted against Bork. One analyst put the cost of the anti-Bork media effort at an unprecedented $15 million.

Although the American Bar Association rated Bork "well qualified," the ACLU bluntly called him "unfit." Senator Kennedy, who led the fight against the conservative jurist, charged apocalyptically that confirmation of Bork would lead to an America where women would have back-alley abortions, blacks would sit at segregated lunch counters, police would "break down citizens' doors in midnight raids," and the doors of the federal courts would be "shut on the fingers of millions of citizens." The Supreme Court correspondent of the *Boston Globe*, the senator's hometown newspaper, wrote that Kennedy "shamelessly twisted Bork's world view."[189]

Bork's nomination dominated the national political agenda in the late summer and early fall of 1987. His five days of testimony before the Senate Judiciary Committee were nationally televised. Former President Gerald Ford personally introduced the nominee to the committee, causing former President Jimmy Carter to send a letter stating his opposition. One hundred and ten witnesses appeared for and against Bork during two weeks of hearings. After the Democrat-controlled Judiciary Committee refused to recommend Bork, the Senate then voted 58 to 42 against confirmation. Shortly thereafter, Reagan nominated and secured Senate confirmation of Anthony Kennedy, a low-key moderate conservative. He selected Kennedy after his earlier choice, Judge Douglas Ginsburg, withdrew his name when it was revealed that he had smoked marijuana as a Harvard student and law professor (something that the FBI, in its background check of Ginsburg, had inexplicably failed to uncover).

Iran-Contra

The Iran-Contra affair had its origins in two typical impulses of Ronald Reagan. The first was humanitarian—to free the handful of America hostages held by terrorists in Lebanon. The second was ideological—to support the anti-Communist resistance in Nicaragua where a Marxist regime threatened freedom in Central America. But exchanging arms for hostages contradicted the Administration's stated policy of not giving in to the demands of terrorists or dealing with a state like Iran that supported terrorist groups. NSC staffers, however, believed that moderate elements in Iran could help facilitate the release of the Americans in Lebanon, and Reagan, eager to free Americans held captive, approved an Iranian initiative at the end of 1985. His cabinet split over his decision, with Attorney General Meese and CIA Director Casey in favor and Secretary of State Shultz and Defense Secretary Weinberger opposed.

At about the same time, Congress passed a series of amendments denying any U.S. support either "directly or indirectly" to the Contras. Responding to the President's oft-expressed wish to help what he called Nicaragua's "freedom fighters," Administration lawyers decided that the National Security Council staff did not fall under the congressional prohibition. So the pro-Contra effort was shifted from the CIA to the NSC under the direction of National Security Adviser John Poindexter and NSC staffer Oliver North. Acting without the President's knowledge, North illegally diverted profits from Iranian arms sales to the Contras.

By mid-November 1986, Washington was awash with rumors about the Iran initiative, fueled by testimony before Congress by CIA Director Bill Casey and a presidential news conference during which Reagan said erroneously that no third country was involved in the transactions (Israel was in fact the middle man in the arms sales between the U.S. and Iran). On Friday morning, November 21, Ed Meese met in the Oval Office with President Reagan and said that because nobody seemed to know the whole story, "it was

Ronald Reagan Library

President Reagan and Ed Meese at the November 1986
Iran-Contra press conference.

important that someone do an overview" so that the Administration
could "give a straightforward account to the American people."[190]
The President asked Meese to undertake such an inquiry, confirm-
ing that in a crisis, Reagan turned to his trustworthy adviser.

Meese asked Brad Reynolds and John Richardson to assemble a
documentary record while he and Charles Cooper interviewed as
many of the principal players as they could. "Find the truth," Meese
told his colleagues, "and tell the truth. There is going to be no cov-
erup."[191] In one weekend the Meese team conducted a remarkable
fact-finding review that uncovered all the essential elements of
Iran-Contra. The diversion of funds from the Iranian initiative to
support the freedom fighters of Nicaragua, Meese reported, was

not done out of "cupidity, self-gain, or other corrupt motives." Rather, public officials, angered at what they viewed as the selling out of brave men fighting for democracy in Central America, took extreme steps that damaged the Administration and "resulted in great harm to the individuals themselves."[192] As for the President's culpability, every official inquiry into Iran-Contra, including special prosecutor Lawrence Walsh's eight-year multi-million-dollar marathon, concluded the same thing: There was no credible evidence that the President authorized or was aware of the diversion of the profits from the Iran arms sales to assist the Contras.[193]

Critical lessons were learned from Iran-Contra, Meese said, and they were incorporated into governmental policy by President Reagan. Operations, including covert actions, should not be run out of the White House. Clandestine operations, especially those entailing high risk, must be reviewed frequently by the President and the National Security Council. When sharp differences exist between Congress and the executive branch over goals and policies, "hostility may cloud judgment on either side." In such instances, said Meese, "good faith is needed if the national interest is to be served." Finally, "the greatest threat to constitutional government and the liberties of the U.S. citizen," argued Meese, "comes not from those involved in affairs like Iran-Contra but a congressionally-initiated institution—the independent counsel.[194] (Congress finally closed down the Office of the Independent Counsel, but not until 1999, after the impeachment of President Bill Clinton.)

Ed Meese knew only too well how much the IC threatened an individual's liberty. In May 1987 he again became the target of a probe when Senator Joseph Biden and Congressman Peter Rodino (both Democrats) urged the appointment of an independent counsel to investigate whether Meese—while serving in the White House in the early 1980s—had improperly received anything of value for asking the Army to consider a contract application of Wedtech, a New York City military contractor. That was the *stated* reason for demanding an investigation. The real reason was that Attorney General Edwin Meese III was the leader of a largely successful campaign to change the legal and even, it may be argued, the social culture of America. He was slaying or grievously wounding liberal dragons on all sides, including judicial activism, racial preferences, and criminals' rights. He was the moving force behind a dramatic alteration in the federal courts, searching for and finding the brightest conservative lawyers in the land, such as Antonin Scalia, Robert Bork, Richard Posner, Frank Easterbrook, Laurence Silberman, Alex Kozinski, and Ralph Winter. And it was his department that "led nearly every state to adopt tort reforms, and persuaded the Supreme Court to bring back property rights."[195]

He even saved the Chicago futures market from grievous and unnecessary government regulation. When the New York Stock Exchange went into free fall in mid-October 1987—losing nearly 23 percent of its total value on just one day, "Black Monday," October 19—NYSE officials began blaming the Chicago futures market. The crash had started in Chicago, they said, and had spread to New York. Futures products were clearly under-regulated, they claimed, and ought to be brought under the Securities and Exchange Commission.

On the morning of Monday, October 19, before the markets opened, Attorney General Ed Meese took senior assistant Joseph A. Morris aside and said he was worried that the crisis might be used to impose draconian "emergency" regulations on the market. The

Meese Family Collection

Meese with daughter Dana and wife Ursula, 1985.

consequences for capital formation, the nation's economy, and the well-being of ordinary Americans would be serious and long-lasting. What was needed, Meese said, was time. If controls could be stalled and the markets left free to operate, "stabilization and a rebound were sure to follow."[196]

As chairman of the Cabinet Council on Domestic Policy, Meese had asked to see President Reagan at noon. If the President were persuaded that the Meese-led council was on top of the emergency, it and not pro-regulators would develop the Administration's response. The key, Morris recalls Meese saying, was to show that the market crisis should be treated as a matter of "broad *domestic* rather than of merely *economic* policy." In just a few hours, a draft presidential decision document was prepared for Meese, who edited it and left for the White House. He returned to Justice authorized by President Reagan to take the lead in dealing with the market crash.

While others were demanding controls and that the government *do* something, Morris remembers, Ed Meese remained calm and waited for the market to correct itself. His judgment was quickly confirmed. The next day, October 20, the Dow rose over 100 points and a day later it climbed another 187 points, pushing the Dow back over the 2,000 mark. Academic studies and congressional hearings later established that Chicago futures trading had not triggered the New York equities crash. Government restraint was proven to be the correct course. "Ed Meese was right on Black Monday, 1987," says Joe Morris, "freedom works."[197]

A year later, in a gargantuan 814-page report, independent counsel James McKay concluded there was "no evidence Mr. Meese had acted from motivation for personal gain" in the Wedtech matter and stated there would be no indictment. But McKay went on at great length to critique Ed Meese's alleged improprieties (such as supporting the idea of a $1 billion Middle East pipeline that was never built or funded). McKay did not offer an apology for the massive and illegal leaks, apparently from his office, that had encouraged partisans to post "Meese Is A Pig" posters all over Washington and to lob rhetorical stink bombs at Meese ("Mr. Meese has become the crown jewel of the sleaze factor in Reagan administration history," declared one senator).

As part of the frenzy created, the media staked out the Meese home in northern Virginia each morning starting at about 6 a.m.

One morning Meese left at 5:45 a.m., before the press arrived. When Ursula backed out of the Meese garage at about 8:30 a.m., and drove past the assembled cameras and reporters, a woman reporter jumped onto her car and began pounding on the trunk, yelling, "He's in the trunk! I know he's in the trunk!" A shocked Ursula stopped the car, opened up the trunk, and showed her that Ed wasn't there. According to Ursula, some of the reporters said, "We really hate doing this, but it's our job."[198]

In the middle of the year-long sleaze campaign, Ed Meese showed his true grit by reiterating in a national television interview that he would not capitulate to a "lynch mob," "media barrages," and "politically motivated attacks."[199] Through it all, the President stuck by his right-hand man, making a point of putting his arm around Meese's shoulder in the press briefing room of the White House when reporters and cameras were present. On another occasion, when asked to comment on the allegations about the Attorney General, he responded, "If Ed Meese is not a good man, there are no good men."[200]

Although much of the criticism was flagrantly partisan, there were some notable exceptions. In the summer of 1988, shortly before the release of the independent counsel's report, Attorney General Meese flew to Minneapolis to address the annual meeting of the National District Attorneys Association. He was introduced by Richard M. Daley, state's attorney for Cook County, son of the late Mayor Richard Daley of Chicago, and a rapidly rising star of the Democratic Party in the Midwest. (Daley was elected mayor of Chicago the following year.) "It is my honor," said Daley," to introduce a man who is the best friend that the nation's law enforcement agencies have ever had at the Department of Justice and is the

greatest Attorney General in the history of the United States."[201]
Daley's liberal praise was public recognition of Ed Meese's produc-
tive campaign to build better relations between federal, state, and
local law enforcement agencies, including the creation of an Office
of Liaison Services.

Meese had already told the President that he intended to leave
the Administration before the end of the term. And so, saying he
been "completely vindicated" by the McKay report, he announced
on July 5, 1988, that he would step down as the seventy-fifth Attorney General of the United States. "He was a darn good attorney general," the President told reporters after the announcement,
adding, "I'm going to miss him."[202] In a formal statement, Reagan
said that Ed Meese could "look back with great satisfaction" on the
contribution he had made as Attorney General. And he stated why
Meese had been so important to him personally: "His gift for developing and succinctly summarizing policy options is one of the most
unique I have encountered in my experience in government."[203]

Even such an encomium did not satisfy the President. In his
weekly radio address a few days later, Reagan called Ed Meese "a
public servant of dedication and integrity, who's been a close friend
for over 20 years." The President pointed out that as Attorney
General, Meese had worked for stricter sentencing of criminals
and greater resources for drug enforcement and to fight organized
crime. In a system usually focused on the criminal, Reagan said, Ed
Meese "never forgot the victims of crime or their rights." He "led
our effort" to appoint highly qualified federal judges who would
crack down on crime and faithfully interpret the Constitution, said
Reagan. Meese led the Justice Department's aggressive defense of
civil rights; "in fact," said the President, "this administration has

achieved more convictions for civil rights violations than any previous administration." As for terrorism, Attorney General Meese "worked closely with our allies" to detect, apprehend and prosecute those "who wage war on innocent members of free societies." And the President stressed Ed Meese's role as a "central figure" in the campaign against illegal drugs in his capacity as chairman of the National Drug Policy Board.[204] Few departing cabinet members have received such acclaim from the chief executive of the nation.

On August, 5, 1988, shortly before he left Justice, Ed Meese was given a rousing going-away party by department employees who presented him with plaques and gifts, including a tomahawk and an inoperative hand grenade—presumably for defense purposes only. With applause echoing in his ears, he returned to his office where among half-packed boxes and bare walls he dealt with a few remaining items on his desk. At close to 8 p.m., the phone rang—it was the White House budget director checking on some of the details of the President's legislative package before Congress. When an aide left the office a little later, he looked back to see the Attorney General still at work.[205]

Chapter VI

PRESERVING THE LEGACY

~~

When they leave office, most attorneys general join a prestigious law firm in Washington or New York City as a "rainmaker" or become the head of a major corporation or trade association at a high six-figure salary. They look forward to serving on a board or two, making the occasional speech, and perhaps lowering their golf score. Not so Ed Meese, who wants to be where he can make a difference defending the written Constitution and bringing justice to the people.

In December 1987, Senator Bob Dole spoke to the President's Club of The Heritage Foundation and said something that hit Heritage President Ed Feulner hard: While "we don't know who's going to be in the Oval Office in January 1989," Dole said, "we know it's not going to be Ronald Reagan." Heritage had been Reagan's favorite think tank for eight years—could it survive without him? "We decided it was time," Feulner recalled, "to return to our congressional roots and help move policy in a conservative direction through the legislative branch."[206] At the same time, Heritage was eager to help preserve the Reagan legacy.

With a $1 million grant from the Grover M. Hermann Foundation and another $1.5 million raised by an endowment committee headed by Ambassador Holland H. (Holly) Coors, Heritage established the Ronald Reagan Chair in Public Policy in the early spring of 1989. It was the only Reagan chair in America formally approved by the former president. "We asked ourselves," Feulner remembers: "'Who is there to carry on the Reagan tradition and fill the Reagan chair?' One name jumped out — Ed Meese."

"My knowledge of the experience of other think tanks," explains Feulner, "was that big names — cabinet members and so forth — might be nice for their luster, but they tend to be prima donnas. They are not team players. We wanted someone who was the incarnation of the Reagan spirit on issues and who could work with us as a member of the Heritage team."[207]

In June 1990, at the annual Heritage board meeting and public policy seminar, Edwin Meese III was formally named The Heritage Foundation's Ronald Reagan Fellow in Public Policy. (Meese had joined Heritage in 1988 as a Distinguished Fellow shortly after leaving Justice.) President Reagan warmly endorsed the creation of a Reagan Chair and its first occupant, saying, "I feel strongly that Heritage is the perfect place for the Reagan Chair, and I am very pleased to be able to salute my old friend, Ed Meese, who is to be commended for many years of dedicated service to our country, and is most deserving of this special honor." Reagan went on to praise the Foundation's contributions to his Administration. "You [were] an invaluable resource on key issues," Reagan said, "such as tax cuts, reducing government spending, SDI, supporting freedom in Grenada, Nicaragua, Eastern Europe — whenever I needed Heritage, you were there." Conceding that he might sound "a little

The White House

Meese with President Ronald Reagan and former Presidents Gerald Ford, Jimmy Carter, and Richard Nixon, 1981.

mystical," the seventy-nine-year-old statesman repeated one of his favorite themes: Americans "were pre-ordained to carry the torch of freedom for the whole world. One of the places that torch has burned most brightly has been at The Heritage Foundation, as it always will."[208]

In an address entitled "The Reagan Legacy," Ed Meese seconded his former boss, saying that "perhaps more than any other organization in Washington," Heritage was instrumental in developing the legacy. *Mandate for Leadership*, for example, was "the only document that the President asked every cabinet member to read. It was distributed literally on the first day of the administration." Meese pointed out that Heritage contributed people as well as ideas, and it always maintained its "intellectual integrity," serving as "a valuable critic" whenever government policy headed in the wrong direction.[209]

After mentioning the record economic expansion at home and the "triumph of democracy" around the world during the 1980s, Meese stressed the former president's spiritual legacy, starting with how he "restored the confidence of a nation which had been badly shattered." Reagan did so by restoring Americans' faith in "the vital credos of personal, political, and economic liberty." He also provided perspective about our history and our values such as individual liberty, free enterprise, and "peace through strength." And he provided a vision of "where America was going, where it should go, and how to get there." The new Ronald Reagan Fellow assured the audience that Heritage would lead the way in the effort "to preserve, protect, and perpetuate the Reagan Legacy." And to do that, Meese concluded, "We must affirm the principles of limited government and federalism that are the core of our constitutional republic."[210]

Every officer and trustee of The Heritage Foundation agrees they made the right choice in Ed Meese. "Ed has been absolutely stellar as a team player," Feulner says. "He has the gravitas to pull together people and organizations. His manifold appearances and speeches have influenced countless people. He is absolutely indispensable to the   conservative movement."[211] Among Meese's Heritage highlights:

• He co-authored with Robert Moffit, the foundation's director of domestic policy studies, a major 1996 study on how to win the war on crime, even in cities like New York. The steps: concentrate available resources on high-crime areas and repeat offenders, get officers out from behind desks and back on the street, improve recruitment and pay standards, aggressively recruit police officers from the military and the neighborhoods they serve, and make every officer—from top to bottom—responsible for reducing crime. Rudolph Giuliani implemented most of the above as mayor of New York City from 1993-2001, reducing overall crime by 57 percent and murder by 65 percent in the nation's largest city.

• Ed Meese emerged, in the wake of September 11, 2001, as perhaps the nation's leading authority on the necessary equilibrium between security and liberty in the war against terrorism. Just one month after the terrorist attacks, he wrote, along with Kim Holmes, Heritage's vice president for foreign policy, that the Bush Administration's anti-terrorism legislation (the USA PATRIOT Act) for the most part struck "the right balance between privacy and security." It would update wiretapping laws to conform to changing technologies, permit information sharing between law enforcement and intelligence agencies, and keep classified information from leaking in court. The fact is, Meese said, that "liberty depends on security and freedom as we know it in America depends on eliminating the threat of terrorism from our lives." Americans "will never be free," warned Meese, "so long as terrorists threaten our homeland." It would be ironic, he said, if "an inordinate fear of losing some rights" denied the nation the tools it needed to stop that which "would doom the Constitution—the scourge of terrorism."[212]

• Meese helped launch, in 2000, the Foundation's Center for Legal and Judicial Studies, serving as its chairman while Heritage senior fellow Todd Gaziano assumed the duties of director. The Center conducts "moot court" sessions for lawyers who will argue cases before the Supreme Court and disseminates "Supreme Court Alerts" explaining the likely impact of Court decisions within an

The Meese Family, 2002, (clockwise from top left): Michael, Marko, Ed, Ursula, Brian, Dana, Alec, Allison, Rebecca, and Ramona.

hour after they are handed down. Two years later the Center added former assistant independent counsel Paul Rosenzweig as senior legal research fellow to inventory the rapidly growing list of federal crimes and propose how to counter the trend to criminalize activities that are "neither criminal nor the federal government's business."[213] Last year, author James Swanson joined the Center as senior legal scholar, focusing on judicial nominations and constitutional law.

• Meese hosts a monthly luncheon meeting of the Public Interest Law Group, which includes heads of freedom-based public interest organizations, Justice Department officials, senior congressional staffers, and other members of Washington's legal community. (As mentioned earlier, as chief of staff to Governor Reagan, he helped lay the foundation, in 1972 and 1973, for the first freedom-based public interest law firm—the Pacific Legal Foundation.) PILG participants discuss Supreme Court decisions, judicial nominations, Justice Department actions, pending legislation on Capitol Hill, and legal cases of a national or constitutional significance. Vice president Roger Clegg of the Center for Equal Opportunity, a regular at the monthly PILG meetings, says that "only Ed could have brought it about" because he is "trusted and respected by a whole variety of organizations." Meese also chairs the Legal Strategy Forum, which twice a year brings together CEOs of public interest law groups, federal judges, legal scholars, and jurists to discuss the major legal issues and trends within a constitutional, freedom-based framework. Here again, says Clegg, the essential catalyst is Ed Meese.[214] He was the impetus for the research and writing of *Bringing Justice to the People: The Story of the Freedom-Based Public Interest Law Movement*, edited by Lee Edwards and praised by Kenneth Starr, former solicitor general of the United States, as "a vitally important book chronicling the restoration of reason to government and the reassertion of freedom in the legal sphere."[215]

• With Heritage as his bully pulpit and the Constitution as his guiding star, Meese addresses critical national issues such as the urgent need for tort reform ("these outrageously excessive fees are worse than unethical—they represent a grave danger to the American political system"); the dangers of overreacting to alleged abuses of fundamental liberties in the USA PATRIOT Act ("most of the proposals for reform mistake the appearance of potential problems and abuse ... with the reality of no abuse at all"); the importance of the Defense of Marriage Act ("to guard the states' liberty to determine marriage policy in accord with the principles of federalism, society . . . must prevent the institution from being redefined out of existence or abolished altogether"); and Senate Democrats' obstruction of President Bush's judicial nominees ("the minority in the Senate is using the filibuster in an unprecedented manner to prevent the confirmation of highly qualified judges").[216]

• He sets the goals of the Center for Legal and Judicial Studies, which for 2005 include providing legal and other advice to Members of Congress who are interested in getting rid of the filibuster in judicial selection, obtaining reauthorization of the sunset provisions of the USA PATRIOT Act, and blocking passage of the Law of the Sea Treaty. He oversees the burgeoning publishing arm of the Center for Legal and Judicial Studies and the B. Kenneth Simon Center for American Studies, directed by political historian Matthew Spalding. Leading the list of 2005 books is *The Heritage Guide to the Constitution*, edited by Spalding and David Forte, which includes some 180 essays on every aspect of the Constitution. Ed Meese is chairman of the five-member advisory board for the *Guide*. "We believe," says Meese, "that *The Heritage Guide to the Constitution* will become as important as Joseph Story's 19th century classic *Commentaries on the Constitution*."

At the same time, Ed Meese remains a Visiting Distinguished Fellow at the Hoover Institution at Stanford University, where he worked on his papers and the gubernatorial papers of Ronald Reagan, and is a member of the board of directors of the Landmark Legal Foundation, the Intercollegiate Studies Institute, and the Capital Research Center. He is co-chairman of the board of governors of the Reagan Ranch, which is administered by Young America's Foundation. He has also been a Distinguished Senior

Heritage Foundation President Edwin J. Feulner and Meese present the
Clare Boothe Luce Award to former President Reagan, 1998.

Fellow at the University of London's Institute of United States
Studies; a founding trustee of the Ronald Reagan Presidential Library; president of the Reagan Alumni Association; president of
the Council for National Policy, whose several hundred members
constitute the conservative movement's leading movers and shak-
ers; and president of the Philadelphia Society, the nation's most
respected organization of conservative intellectuals.

He served for eight years on George Mason University's Board of
Visitors, six of them as "rector" or chairman. Meese was no figure-

head in the latter position: The Board of Visitors is the legal governing body of the university with overall responsibility for proper management of the institution. Among the university's achievements during Meese's tenure ending in 2004 were the rise of the law school to "a top tier level," the creation of the School of Public Policy, and the recruitment of outstanding faculty to the department of economics.

He is one of the most sought after conservative speakers in the nation. In just the first part of last December, according to his Heritage assistant Amber Streit, Ed Meese received forty speaking requests and invitations. Unusual, even for the peripatetic Meese, was his dual appearance at Hillsdale College in mid-October 2004. A very concerned Larry Arnn, Hillsdale's president, telephoned Ed Meese on Thursday, October 14, to say that William F. Buckley, Jr., the main speaker for Saturday evening—just two days away—had fallen ill and was obliged to cancel. The only person of equal caliber that Arnn could think of on such short notice was Meese—already scheduled to speak at Hillsdale the following Tuesday. Arnn realized that it was a terrible imposition, but would Ed be willing to fill in for Bill Buckley at the last moment? Without hesitation but with the promise of private transportation, Meese said he would. When he returned home on Sunday, Ursula asked him how his speech went. "Okay," her husband replied. On Monday the Meeses flew to Michigan where Ed again spoke to a Hillsdale audience and received a standing ovation. "You know," said President Arnn to Ursula, "we've only had three standing ovations since I've been here—the last one was Saturday night when Ed spoke."[217]

It is exceedingly embarrassing to the self-effacing Meese, but wherever he goes these days he is acclaimed. When about one

Chas Geer

Since 1990, Meese has served as The Heritage Foundation's
Ronald Reagan Fellow in Public Policy.

hundred members of the Reagan Administration were invited to
the White House after Ronald Reagan's death in June 2004, and
remarks were made by such luminaries as George Shultz, William
Clark, Martin Anderson, and Peggy Noonan, the person who received the warmest applause from the assemblage was Ed Meese.

"Ed's most important legacy," says Martin Anderson, "is that he helped the man who changed the world." The two other members of the White House troika are unanimous in their appraisal of Ed Meese's contribution to the Reagan presidency: "Indispensable," says James Baker. "Ronald Reagan couldn't have made it without Ed," says Michael Deaver. "He's clearly *the* standard bearer of the Reagan Revolution," says William Clark. "He can bring together conservatives of every kind," says Ed Feulner; "no wonder conservatives around the country affectionately call Ed the Godfather." "If he can help," says Lois Haight, "there is no job too small, no effort too great, no place he will not go, if he can lend his name, his reputation, his prestige, or just his strong hands and stout heart." "He's there, always," says Ursula of her husband of forty-five years.[218]

At seventy-three, Ed Meese maintains a daily schedule of speaking, writing, meeting, and advising that would severely test the resources of someone half his age. Heritage executive vice president Phil Truluck suggested a couple of years ago that Meese ought to slow down: "And he did—cutting out paid speeches."[219] He moves quietly and efficiently from task to task. He puts those around him at ease with a smile and a slice of humor. He crisply sums up the salient points at a meeting or conference. He moves audiences with personal stories of working beside Ronald Reagan. He takes the time to counsel young people at every opportunity, encouraging them to consider a career of public service. Like St. Paul—whom he likes to quote—he continues to fight the good fight, to run the race, to keep the faith with his eye on the final prize.

Summing up the 1980s—which launched the Age of Reagan in which we still live—the political scientist Andrew E. Busch wrote that they were a decade of economic liberty, a decade of political liberty, and a decade of global liberty. "In almost every particular," Busch said, "Reagan pursued a course calculated to make America and the world more free and more capable of sustaining freedom."[220]

Ed Meese pursues a similar course, seeing it as his mission to protect the founding principles of America and to preserve the shining legacy of the President whom he served so well for so long.

The End

Notes

~

Introduction

[1] Lou Cannon, "Reagan Moves to Cut Costs by Reorganizing," *The Washington Post*, February 28, 1980; for another version of Reagan on Meese, see "The Return of Mr. Fix-It," *Time*, December 8, 1986.

[2] Telephone interview with James A. Baker, November 18, 2004.

[3] Interview with Michael K. Deaver, November 11, 2004.

[4] *Ibid.*

[5] Telephone interview with William P. Clark, November 26, 2004.

[6] Edwin Meese III, *With Reagan: The Inside Story* (Washington, D.C.: Regnery Gateway, 1992), p. 36.

[7] Allan H. Ryskind, "Reagan's Greatest Success as Governor," *Human Events*, June 28, 2004, p. 16. Lou Cannon, *Governor Reagan: His Rise to Power* (New York: Public Affairs, 2003), p. 359.

[8] Martin Anderson, *Revolution* (San Diego: Harcourt Brace Jovanovich, 1988), pp. 224, 233.

[9] Meese, *With Reagan*, p. 318.

[10] Lou Cannon, *President Reagan: The Role of a Lifetime* (New York: Public Affairs, 2000), p. 802.

[11] Interview with T. Kenneth Cribb, Jr., December 8, 2004.

[12] Remarks by Attorney General Edwin Meese III, before the American Bar Association, July 9, 1985, reprinted in *The Great Debate: Interpreting Our Written*

Constitution (The Federalist Society, 1991), pp. 9-10.

[13] William J. Brennan, Jr., essay in *Views from the Bench: The Judiciary and Constitutional Politics* (New York: Chatham House Publishers, 1985). Frankfurter quote in James Q. Wilson, *American Government* (Lexington, Mass.: D.C. Heath & Company, 1980), p. 398. Telephone interview with Douglas Kmiec, December 14, 2004.

[14] "The Law of the Constitution," remarks by Attorney General Edwin Meese III, Tulane University, October 21, 1986, reprinted in *Who Speaks for the Constitution? The Debate Over Interpretive Authority* (The Federalist Society, 1992).

[15] Meese, *With Reagan*, p. 244.

[16] *Ibid.*, 245.

[17] *Ibid.*, 300.

[18] Interview with Lee Liberman Otis, December 13, 2004. Interview with T. Kenneth Cribb, Jr., December 8, 2004.

[19] Statement by President Ronald Reagan on "The Independent Counsel's Report on Edwin Meese III," September 20, 1984, *Presidential Papers of Ronald Reagan*, 1984, p. 1330.

[20] Douglas W. Kmiec, *The Attorney General's Lawyer: Inside the Meese Justice Department* (New York: Praeger, 1992), pp. 13-15. "Meese the Ripper," *The Wall Street Journal*, March 7, 1984.

[21] Kmiec, *The Attorney General's Lawyer*, pp. 194, 199.

[22] Al Kamen and Howard Kurtz, "Meese Partially Achieved Conservative Goals; Attorney General Seen as Force in Shifting Political Debate, Reshaping U.S. Judiciary," *The Washington Post*, July 6, 1988.

[23] "Who Should've Been the President's Men?" *The Wall Street Journal*, April 6, 1988.

[24] Remarks by William Bradford Reynolds, Edwin J. Feulner, Caspar Weinberger, Judge Lois Haight, "A Tribute to Edwin Meese III," Mayflower Hotel, Washington, D.C., March 26, 1998.

[25] Interviews with Peter Hannaford, October 28, 2004; Jeffrey Bell (telephone), October 28, 2004; Pendleton James (telephone), October 10, 2004; Charles Cooper, November 4, 2004; Richard Wirthlin (telephone), October 25, 2004; Theodore Olson, October 20, 2004; John Richardson, October 8, 2004; Mark Levin, October 8, 2004.

[26] Ronald Reagan, as cited in "A Tribute to Edwin Meese III," March 26, 1998, Washington, D.C., and based on the recollection of T. Kenneth Cribb, Jr., p. 5

[27] Interview with Virginia Thomas, December 17, 2004.

Chapter I

[28] Herb Michelson, "Ed Meese: Old Fashioned, Self-Effacing Reagan Aide," *The Sacramento Bee*, August 10, 1980.

[29] Bob Schieffer and Gary Paul Gates, *The Acting President* (New York: E.P. Dutton, 1989), pp. 34-35.

[30] Kate Coleman, "The Roots of Ed Meese," *Los Angeles Times Magazine*, May 4, 1986, p. 3.

[31] *Ibid.*

[32] *Ibid.*, p. 8.

[33] Interview with Edwin Meese III, December 21, 2004.

[34] Coleman, "The Roots of Ed Meese," p. 4.

[35] Interview with Edwin Meese III, July 8, 2004.

[36] Interview with Edwin Meese III, December 21, 2004.

[37] Coleman, "The Roots of Ed Meese," p. 5.

[38] Interview with Ursula Meese, January 5, 2005.

[39] *Ibid.*

[40] Michelson, "Ed Meese: Old Fashioned, Self-Effacing Reagan Aide."

[41] Diane Ravitch, *The Troubled Crusade* (New York: Basic Books, 1983), p. 191.

[42] *Ibid.*, p. 203.

[43] Schieffer and Gates, *The Acting President*, p. 36.

[44] Coleman, "The Roots of Ed Meese," p. 5.

[45] Schieffer and Gates, *The Acting President*, p. 38.

[46] Coleman, "The Roots of Ed Meese," p. 6.

[47] Michelson, "Ed Meese: Old Fashioned, Self-Effacing Reagan Aide."

[48] *Ibid.*

[49] Interview with Edwin Meese III, July 8, 2004. Excerpted from Meese contribution to *Recollections of Reagan: A Portrait of Ronald Reagan*, edited by Peter Hannaford (New York: William Morrow and Company, 1987), p. 109.

Chapter II

[50] Lee Edwards, *Reagan: A Political Biography* (Houston, Tex.: Nordland Publishing, 1981), p. 127.

[51] Gary G. Hamilton and Nicole Woolsey Biggart, *Governor Reagan, Governor Brown: A Sociology of Power* (New York: Columbia University Press, 1984), p. 165.

[52] "Reagan's Real Record in California," *U.S. News & World Report*, February 9, 1976, p. 15.

[53] Hamilton and Biggart, *Governor Reagan, Governor Brown*, p. 166.

[54] "The Story of Ronald Reagan: Governor of Nation's Biggest State," *U.S. News & World Report*, January 2, 1967, p. 35.

[55] Schieffer and Gates, *The Acting President*, p. 39.

[56] Telephone interview with William P. Clark, November 26, 2004.

[57] Memorandum from Ed Meese to Bill Clark, October 16, 1968, "Position on Campus Disorders," Papers of Edwin J. Meese III, Ronald Reagan Governor's Papers, Ronald Reagan Presidential Library, Simi Valley, California.

[58] Kiron K. Skinner, Annelise Anderson, and Martin Anderson, eds., *Reagan: A Life in Letters* (New York: Free Press, 2003), p. 583.

[59] Telephone interview with William P. Clark, November 26, 2004.

[60] Interview with Michael K. Deaver, November 11, 2004.

[61] Cannon, *Governor Reagan: His Rise to Power*, pp. 327-328.

[62] Michelson, "Ed Meese: Old Fashioned: Self-Effacing Reagan Aide."

[63] For William Bagley quote, see Michelson, "Ed Meese: Old Fashioned, Self-Effacing Reagan Aide." For Bob Moretti quote, see Schieffer and Gates, *The Acting President*, p. 45.

[64] "Reagan's Top Staff Aide," *California Journal*, June 1970, p. 156.

[65] Hamilton and Biggart, *Governor Reagan, Governor Brown*, p. 175.

[66] *Ibid.*

[67] Nicole Woolsey Biggart, "Management Style as Strategic Interaction: The Case of Governor Ronald Reagan," *The Journal of Applied Behavioral Science*, Vol. 17, No. 3 (1981), p. 304.

[68] For Meese comments on welfare eligibility, see minutes of Cabinet-Staff Meeting, November 22, 1968, Papers of Edwin Meese III, Ronald Reagan Governor's Papers, Ronald Reagan Presidential Library, Simi Valley, California. For Ronald Reagan memo on assistance programs, see Cannon, *Governor Reagan*, p. 349.

[69] *Ibid.*

[70] Steven F. Hayward, *The Age of Reagan: The Fall of the Old Liberal Order, 1964-1980* (Roseville, Calif.: Forum (Prima Publishing), 2001), p. 241.

[71] Ronald Reagan to Kenneth Fisher, circa late 1970s, reprinted in Skinner et al., eds., *Reagan: A Life in Letters*, p. 363.

[72] Charles D. Hobbs, "How Ronald Reagan Governed California," *National Re-*

view, January 17, 1975, p. 39.

73 Cannon, *Governor Reagan*, pp. 358-359.

74 Ryskind, "Reagan's Greatest Success as Governor," p. 16.

75 Hamilton and Biggart, *Governor Reagan, Governor Brown*, p. 166.

76 Cannon, *Governor Reagan*, pp. 386, 389.

Chapter III

77 *Ibid.*, p. 396.

78 Ronald Reagan quotation taken from a news release of the Office of Governor Ronald Reagan, December 4, 1974.

79 Interview with Ursula Meese, January 5, 2005.

80 Peter Hannaford, *The Reagans: A Political Portrait* (New York: Coward-Mc-Cann, 1983), p. 63.

81 "A President 'in Jeopardy,'" *Newsweek*, May 17, 1976, p. 22.

82 Cannon, *Governor Reagan*, p. 430.

83 Hannaford, *The Reagans*, p. 131.

84 Lee Edwards, *The Essential Ronald Reagan* (Lanham, Md.: Rowman & Littlefield, 2005), p. 76.

85 Edmund Morris, *Dutch: A Memoir of Ronald Reagan* (New York: Random House, 1999), p. 401.

86 Cannon, *Governor Reagan*, p. 433.

87 Hayward, *The Age of Reagan*, p. 613.

88 *Ibid.*, 616. Edwards, *The Essential Ronald Reagan*, p. 77.

89 Telephone interview with Jay A. Parker, January 6, 2005.

90 Telephone interview with Richard Huffman, February 7, 2005.

91 Interview with Edwin Meese III, September 21, 2004. Cannon, *Governor Reagan*, p. 449.

92 Interview with Edwin Meese III, September 21, 2004.

93 For the Reagan quote about Ed Meese, see Anne Edwards, *The Reagans: Portrait of a Marriage* (New York: St Martin's Press, 2003), p. 147. For the Reagan quote about John Sears, see Lyn Nofziger in *Reagan: The Man and His Presidency* by Deborah Hart Strober and Gerald S. Strober (Boston: Houghton Mifflin Company, 1998), p. 17. For the Nofziger quote about the Rose Garden, see Cannon, *Governor Reagan*, p. 458.

94 Ronald Reagan, *An American Life* (New York: Simon and Schuster, 1990),

p. 214.

[95] Jeff Greenfield, *The Real Campaign: How the Media Missed the Story of the 1980 Campaign* (New York: Simon and Schuster, 1981), p. 48.

[96] Dick Wirthlin with Wynton C. Hall, *The Greatest Communicator: What Ronald Reagan Taught Me about Politics, Leadership, and Life* (Hoboken, N.J.: John Wiley & Sons, 2004), p. 45.

[97] Michael K. Deaver, *A Different Drummer: My Thirty Years with Ronald Reagan* (New York: HarperCollins, 2001), p. 198.

[98] Mike Wallace in *Recollections of Reagan: A Portrait of Ronald Reagan*, ed., Peter Hannaford (New York: William Morrow, 1997), p. 181.

[99] Greenfield, *The Real Campaign*, p. 160.

[100] Wirthlin, *The Great Communicator*, p. 58.

[101] Lyn Nofziger, *Nofziger* (Washington, D.C.: Regnery Gateway, 1992), p. 242.

[102] Greenfield, *The Real Campaign*, p. 164. Cannon, *Governor Reagan*, p. 475.

[103] "George Bush on His Role as No. 2," *U.S. News & World Report*, July 28, 1980, pp. 23-24. Strober and Strober, *Reagan*, p. 27.

[104] Interview with Pendleton James, November 12, 2004.

[105] *Ibid.*

[106] Interview with Edwin Meese III, September 21, 2004.

[107] Comment of Pendleton James in *The Keys to a Successful Presidency*, edited by Alvin S. Felzenberg (Washington, D.C.: The Heritage Foundation, 2000), p. 51.

[108] Cannon, *Governor Reagan*, p. 477.

[109] Adriana Bosch, *Reagan: An American Story* (New York: TV Books, 2000), p. 125.

[110] I have depended upon two primary sources for the debate about the debate: Lou Cannon, *Governor Reagan*, pp. 500-502; and Rowland Evans and Robert Novak, *The Reagan Revolution* (New York: E. P. Dutton, 1981), p. 82.

[111] Greenfield, *The Real Campaign*, pp. 235-241.

[112] *Ibid.*

[113] Edwards, *The Essential Ronald Reagan*, p. 90.

[114] Wallace Earl Walker and Michael R. Reopel, "Strategies for Governance: Transition and Domestic Policymaking in the Reagan Administration," *Presidential Studies Quarterly*, Vol. 16, No. 4 (Fall 1986), p. 1.

[115] Martin Anderson, *Revolution*, p. 199.

[116] *Ibid.*

[117] Interview with T. Kenneth Cribb, Jr., December 12, 2004.

[118] "A Modest Program," *The Wall Street Journal*, September 22, 1980.

[119] Schieffer and Gates, *The Acting President*, p. 82.

[120] Cannon, *President Reagan: The Role of a Lifetime*, p. 50.

[121] Attributed to Robert Woodruff (1889-1985), chairman of The Coca-Cola Company and Atlanta, Georgia, philanthropist, as his personal creed.

[122] Schieffer and Gates, *The Acting President*, p. 83.

[123] Morris, *Dutch: A Memoir of Ronald Reagan*, p. 420.

[124] Interviews with Baker, November 18, 2004; Deaver, November 11, 2004; and Meese, November 9, 2004.

[125] Oral History of Jack Wrather, September 30, 1982, Bancroft Library Oral History, UC-Berkeley, Hoover Archives, Stanford University, Stanford, California.

[126] Strober and Strober, *Reagan*, p. 65.

[127] Interview with Edwin Meese III, February 22, 2005.

[128] Christian Williams, "Cool Hand Meese, Reagan's Resilient Adjutant," *The Washington Post*, December 11, 1980.

[129] *Ibid.*

[130] *Ibid.*

Chapter IV

[131] Martin Anderson, *Revolution*, p. 232.

[132] Meese, *With Reagan*, p. 130.

[133] Anderson, *Revolution*, pp. 238-239.

[134] Interview with Lyn Nofziger, September 30, 2004.

[135] Meese, *With Reagan*, p. 18. Also see Edwin Meese III, "A Man of Courage," The Heritage Foundation Tribute to Ronald Reagan, July 2004, p. 5.

[136] Anderson, *Revolution*, pp. 94-95.

[137] Meese, *With Reagan*, p. 193.

[138] Anderson, *Revolution*, p. 97.

[139] "Nuclear Facts, Science Fictions," *The New York Times*, March 27, 1983.

[140] Peter Schweizer, *Reagan's War: The Epic Story of His Forty-year Struggle and Final Triumph Over Communism* (New York: Random House, 2002), p. 152. Daniel O. Graham, *Confessions of a Cold Warrior* (Fairfax, Va.: Preview Press, 1995), p. 153.

[141] George J. Church, "The President's Men," *Time*, December 14, 1981.

[142] Bill Bright to Edwin Meese, December 23, 1981; Meese quotation from his remarks to the Congress on the Bible, Papers of Edwin Meese III, Hoover Archives, Stanford University, Stanford, California.

[143] Cannon, *President Reagan*, p. 419.

[144] Meese, *With Reagan*, p. 147.

[145] Louise Sweeney, "Presidential Counselor Ed Meese," *Christian Science Monitor*, August 26, 1982.

[146] *Ibid.*

[147] *Ibid.*

[148] Interview with T. Kenneth Cribb, Jr., December 8, 2004.

[149] Telephone interview with Pendleton James, October 10, 2004.

[150] Interview with Steven Calabresi, February 11, 2005. Interview with Leonard Leo, December 23, 2004. E-mail message from Eugene B. Meyer to Lee Edwards, February 18, 2005.

[151] Interviews with Nofziger, September 30, 2004; Cribb, December 8, 2004. For Meese quote, see Meese, *With Reagan*, p. 25.

[152] Interviews with John Herrington, November 11, 2004, and Pendleton James, November 12, 2004.

[153] Tony Mauro, "The Other Reagan Revolution," *Legal Times*, June 14, 2004.

[154] Meese, *With Reagan*, p. 318.

[155] Lou Cannon, *Governor Reagan*, pp. 721-722. Tony Mauro, "The Other Reagan Revolution."

[156] Ronald Reagan, "Nomination of Edwin Meese III To Be Attorney General of the United States," January 23, 1984, Presidential Papers, 1984.

[157] "The Meese Inquisition," *The Wall Street Journal*, March 1, 1984. Ronald Reagan to Thomas O'Brien, March 22, 1984, in *Reagan: A Life in Letters*, edited by Kiron Skinner, Annelise Anderson and Martin Anderson. (New York: Free Press, 2003), p. 367. Remarks by Ronald Reagan, March 13, 1984, Q and A session with reporters, *Presidential Papers of Ronald Reagan*, 1984, p. 350. Remarks by Ronald Reagan, March 21, 1984, Q and A session with reporters, *Presidential Papers of Ronald Reagan*, 1984, p. 398.

[158] As quoted in Kmiec, *The Attorney General's Lawyer*, p. 5.

[159] "Report of Independent Counsel Concerning Edwin Meese III," Jacob A. Stein, Independent Counsel, September 20, 1984, U.S. Court of Appeals for the District of Columbia Circuit; "About Press Vendettas," *The Wall Street Journal*, October 1, 1984; "Nomination of Edwin Meese III," Hearings before the Commit-

tee on the Judiciary, United States Senate, March 1, 2, 5, and 6, 1984, p. 27.

[160] "A Senator Named Joe," *The Wall Street Journal*, February 4, 1985.

[161] *Ibid.*

[162] John A. Jenkins, "Mr. Power: Attorney General Meese is Reagan's man to lead the conservative charge," *The New York Times Magazine*, October 12, 1986.

[163] David Rogers and Andy Pasztor, "Senate Confirms Meese to Head Justice Agency," *The Wall Street Journal*, February 25, 1985.

Chapter V

[164] Meese, *With Reagan*, pp. 305-306.

[165] Telephone interview with Lois Haight, November 11, 2004.

[166] Meese, *With Reagan*, p. 310.

[167] *Ibid.*, p. 311.

[168] *Ibid.*, p. 312.

[169] *Ibid.*, p. 314.

[170] Andrew Busch, *Ronald Reagan and the Politics of Freedom* (Lanham, Md.: Roman & Littlefield Publishers, 2001), p. 21. Ronald Reagan, "At the Investiture of Chief Justice William H. Rehnquist and Associate Justice Antonin Scalia at the White House, September 26, 1986, Washington, D.C.," in *The Great Debate: Interpreting Our Written Constitution*, p. 55.

[171] Stephen Wermiel, "Meese Contends Supreme Court Opinions in Past Term Often Were Policy Choices," *The Wall Street Journal*, July 10, 1985.

[172] Bruce Fein as quoted in Merrill Hartson, "High Profile Boss," *St. Louis Post-Dispatch*, August 29, 1985.

[173] Kathryn Kahler, "Courts a battleground for conservative agenda," *Newark Star Ledger*, August 25, 1985.

[174] Philip Shenon, "Meese and His New Vision of the Constitution," *The New York Times*, October 14, 1985.

[175] *Ibid.*

[176] Stephen Wermiel, "Two Centuries Later, There Is Hot Debate Over 'Original Intent,'" *The Wall Street Journal*, May 20, 1987.

[177] Edwin Meese III, "The Battle for the Constitution," *Policy Review*, Winter 1985, pp. 32-35 (based on his speech to the Federalist Society, November 15, 1985).

[178] "The Irrepressible Mr. Meese," *The Wall Street Journal*, October 29, 1986.

[179] *Ibid.*

[180] Interview with T. Kenneth Cribb, Jr., December 8, 2004.

[181] *Report to the Attorney General: Religious Liberty Under the Free Exercise Clause,* U.S. Department of Justice, Office of Legal Policy, August 13, 1986, p. iv

[182] Interview with Becky Norton Dunlop, October 18, 2004.

[183] *Up From Dependency: A New National Public Assistance Strategy,* Report to the President by the Domestic Policy Council, December 1986, p. 5; *The Family: Preserving America's Future,* Report to the President from the White House Working Group on the Family, December 1986, p. 5; *The Status of Federalism in America,* A Report of the Working Group on Federalism of the Domestic Policy Council, November 1986, p. 5.

[184] Telephone interview with Steven Calabresi, February 11, 2005.

[185] Sheldon Goldman, "Reagan's Judicial Legacy: Completing the Puzzle and Summing Up," *Judicature,* April/May 1989.

[186] Terry Eastland, "Reagan Justice: Combating Excess, Strengthening the Rule of Law," *Policy Review,* Fall 1988, p. 21.

[187] Goldman, "Reagan's Judicial Legacy."

[188] Interview with T. Kenneth Cribb, Jr., December 8, 2004.

[189] "Reagan Picks Bork, Sparks Liberal Uproar," *The Washington Times,* July 2, 1987. Cannon, *President Reagan,* p. 807.

[190] Meese, *With Reagan,* pp. 296-297.

[191] Interview with Mark Levin, October 8, 2004.

[192] Meese, *With Reagan,* p. 301.

[193] Cannon, *President Reagan,* p. 662.

[194] Meese, *With Reagan,* p. 302.

[195] "Edwin Meese and Beyond," *The Wall Street Journal,* July 8, 1988.

[196] Joseph A. Morris, "The Crash of '87: How Ed Meese Saved the Chicago Futures Markets," published as a "Lincoln Brief" by the Lincoln Legal Foundation, October 1987.

[197] *Ibid.*

[198] Interview with Ursula Meese, January 5, 2005.

[199] Cannon, *President Reagan,* p. 720; "Trial by Sleaze," *The Wall Street Journal,* March 31, 1988; Andy Pasztor, "Meese's Avoidance of Criminal Charges Won't End Justice Department Turmoil," *The Wall Street Journal,* April 4, 1988.

[200] As recalled by T. Kenneth Cribb, Jr., "A Tribute to Edwin Meese III," Mayflower Hotel, Washington. D.C., March 26, 1998.

[201] Richard M. Daley quotation as recalled by Joseph A. Morris in a telephone interview, February 18, 2005.

[202] Kmiec, *The Attorney General's Lawyer*: 199; Andy Pasztor, "Meese Resigns Abruptly, Claims Prosecutor's Report Clears Him," *The Wall Street Journal*, July 6, 1988; Richard Stengel, "Veni, Vidi, Vindicated? Tarnished but unindicted, the Attorney General calls it quits," *Time*, July 18, 1988.

[203] Ronald Reagan, "Statement on the Resignation of Edwin Meese III as Attorney General," July 5, 1988, *Presidential Papers of Ronald Reagan* 1988, p. 900.

[204] Ronald Reagan, "Radio Address to the Nation on the Resignation of Attorney General Meese and the Fight Against Illegal Drugs," July 9, 1988, *Presidential Papers of Ronald Reagan*, 1988, p. 909.

[205] Kmiec, *The Attorney General's Lawyer*, p. 201.

Chapter VI

[206] Lee Edwards, *The Power of Ideas: The Heritage Foundation at 25 Years* (Ottawa, Ill.: Jameson Books, 1997), p. 99.

[207] Interview with Edwin J. Feulner, October 10, 2004.

[208] Ronald Reagan, keynote address at The Heritage Foundation Annual Board Meeting and Public Policy Seminar, Carmel, CA, June 1990.

[209] Edwin Meese III, "The Reagan Legacy," address given at The Heritage Foundation Annual Board Meeting, June 1990.

[210] *Ibid.*

[211] Interview with Edwin J. Feulner, October 10, 2004.

[212] Kim R. Holmes and Edwin Meese III, "The Administration's Anti-Terrorism Package: Balancing Security and Liberty," Heritage Foundation *Backgrounder* No. 1484, October 3, 2001.

[213] Lee Edwards, ed., *Bringing Justice to the People: The Story of the Freedom-Based Public Interest Law Movement* (Washington, D.C.: The Heritage Foundation, 2004), pp. 107-109.

[214] Interview with Roger Clegg, October 12, 2004.

[215] Kenneth W. Starr, back cover, Edwards, *Bringing Justice to the People*.

[216] Edwin Meese III and Paul Rosenzweig, "The Urgent Need for Civil Justice Reform," Knight-Ridder Tribune Wire, May 29, 2002. Edwin Meese III and Paul Rosenzweig, "The SAFE Act Will Not Make Us Safer," Heritage Founation *Legal Memorandum* No. 10, April 30, 2004. Edwin Meese III, "A Shotgun Amendment,"

The Wall Street Journal, March 10, 2004. "Combating Judicial Activism," an interview with Edwin Meese III, *Heritage Members News*, Fall 2004, pp. 4, 10.

[217] E-mail interview with Larry Arnn, February 11, 2005.

[218] Interviews with Martin Anderson, August 24, 2004; James Baker, November 18, 2004.; Michael Deaver,, November 11, 2004; William Clark, November 26, 2004; Edwin Feulner, October 10, 2004; Ursula Meese, January 5, 2005. Quotation of Lois Haight taken from "A Tribute to Edwin Meese III," Mayflower Hotel, Washington, D.C., March 26, 1998.

[219] Interview with Phillip N. Truluck, October 4, 2004.

[220] Busch, *Ronald Reagan and the Politics of Freedom*, p. 253.

INDEX

~

ACKNOWLEDGMENTS

~~

Ever modest, Ed Meese agreed to cooperate in the writing of this biography only after he was persuaded that the book would help preserve the legacy of Ronald Reagan, strengthen the conservative movement, and further the work of The Heritage Foundation. We were a little disingenuous: We were also determined to present the remarkable story of a remarkable Attorney General, presidential counselor, lawyer, teacher, husband, father, and poker player. I have written biographies and profiles about some of the most famous political figures of America, and I am accustomed to tributes. But I have never before encountered such a unanimous chorus of praise and admiration as in my interviews of those who have known Ed Meese, either for a lifetime or for a few years.

I am indebted to Ed and Ursula Meese for allowing me to talk with them on so many occasions about things public and private. I have promised that I will return all the clippings and family photos, including the one of Ed as a very thin crew-cut senior at Oakland High. I am grateful to the following individuals for sharing their recollections and evaluations: Annelise Anderson, Martin Anderson,

James A. Baker, Jeffrey Bell, Robert Bork, Steven Calabresi, William Clark, Roger Clegg, Charles Cooper, Kenneth Cribb, Michael Deaver, Becky Norton Dunlop, Terry Eastland, Edwin Feulner, Todd Gaziano, Lois Haight, Peter Hannaford, John Herrington, Richard Huffman, Cathy Hurlburt, Pendleton James, Douglas Kmiec, Leonard Leo, Mark Levin, John McClaughery, Joseph A. Morris, Lyn Nofziger, Theodore Olson, Lee Liberman Otis, Gary McDowell, Jay Parker, Alfred Regnery, John Richardson, Elizabeth Reid, Bradford Reynolds, Molly Stark, Amber Streit, Ginni Thomas, Phillip Truluck, Caspar Weinberger, and Richard Wirthlin.

The following individuals were most helpful in the area of research: Judith Lihosit, reference librarian, Legal Research Center, University of San Diego; Valorie McClelland, Goodrich Corporation; Ron Plavchan, archivist, Department of Justice; and Barbara Platt, administrative assistant in the Alameda County district attorney's office.

All biographies and histories are collaborative efforts, and I wish to acknowledge in particular the superb research assistance of Matthew Sitman, who accompanied me to the Hoover Archives at Stanford University to inspect the Meese Papers there. I also thank Dan Szy, Samuel Howard, and Rebeccah Ramey for their efficient help here in Washington, D.C., and Nicole Schouten for her long-distance research at the Reagan Presidential Library in California. Also, many thanks go to The Heritage Foundation's outstanding publishing services and editorial teams. Jonathan Larsen, Carolyn Belefski, Teresa Matous, Therese Pennefather, Richard Odermatt, William T. Poole, and Sam Walker all were essential to helping this book take shape. Todd Gaziano read the manuscript and made his usual excellent editorial suggestions.

Finally, I am grateful to Edwin J. Feulner and The Heritage Foundation for their continuing and generous support of my work and for publishing the biography of an inestimable American, Edwin Meese III.

LEE EDWARDS

About the Author

~

Lee Edwards is Distinguished Fellow in Conservative Thought at The Heritage Foundation in Washington, D.C., adjunct professor of politics at The Catholic University of America, and chairman of the Victims of Communism Memorial Foundation. He is the author of 17 books, including *The Conservative Revolution: The Movement that Remade America*; *The Power of Ideas: The Heritage Foundation at Twenty-Five Years*; *Goldwater: The Man Who Made a Revolution*; and *The Essential Ronald Reagan: A Profile in Courage, Justice, and Wisdom*. Edwards and his wife Anne reside in Alexandria, Virginia.